英汉对照世界名著文库

Kim

Kim

吉 姆

[英] 吉卜林 著

符亦文 译

中国书店

图书在版编目(CIP)数据

吉姆 /(英)吉卜林著;符亦文译.—北京:中国书店,
2007.2 (2012.12 重印)
(英汉对照世界名著文库.第 3 辑)
ISBN 978-7-80663-193-5

Ⅰ.①吉… Ⅱ.①吉… ②符… Ⅲ.①英语-汉语-
对照读物 ②长篇小说-英国-现代 Ⅳ.①H319.4:I

中国版本图书馆 CIP 数据核字(2011)第 015183 号

英汉对照世界名著文库(第 3 辑) 吉姆

作　　者:(英)吉卜林
译　　者:符亦文
责任编辑:杨　颖
装帧设计:李艾红
美术编辑:穆　红
文字编辑:赵　晴

出版发行:中 国 书 店
地　　址:北京市宣武区琉璃厂东街 115 号
邮　　编:100050
经　　销:全国新华书店
印　　刷:北京一鑫印务有限责任公司
开　　本:635mm × 940mm　1/16
版　　次:2007 年 2 月第 1 版　2012 年 12 月第 2 次印刷
字　　数:1247 千字
印　　张:108
书　　号:ISBN 978-7-80663-193-5
定　　价:238.40 元 (全 8 册)

出版说明

为给广大英语爱好者提供一套便捷、有效地学习英语的理想读本,我们编辑出版了这套《英汉对照世界名著文库》系列丛书。其中收录了世界文学史上影响最大、价值最高、流传最广的经典名著,采用英汉对照的方式,旨在帮助广大英语爱好者通过读名著来学习英文。该丛书具有以下四个特点:

一、权威主编 质量一流

本丛书由著名翻译家宋兆霖先生担任主编,所选经典名著无论英文还是译文,都具有很高的文学艺术价值。我们试图通过这一努力,改变国内英汉对照名著良莠杂陈、令读者无所适从的现状。

二、一书两用 物超所值

名著是人类智慧的结晶,文辞优美,结构严谨,具有巨大的思想和艺术魅力。本丛书采用左英右汉的对照形式,帮助读者对照学习。使读者既可以阅读世界名著、陶冶情操、提高修养,又可以培养学习兴趣、提高英语读写能力,双重收获,效率倍增。

三、原汁英语 经典名著

本丛书除收录部分英、美等国作家的原著,对于非英语语言的名著,则由国内外知名的英语专家、学者以精准、流畅的英语重新编写,既保留了原著的精华,又使作品变得浅显易懂,从而避免了长篇名著的晦涩难懂。结合通俗、生动的译文,使读者能够准确地把握名著的精髓。

四、精编精释 理想读本

本丛书依照词汇量的多少及语法结构的难易程度,分为易、中、难三大部分,不同的读者既可以按不同的需求选择阅读,也可以由易到难,系统地学习。结合译作者精当的注释,以及相应的词汇表,帮助读者扫除阅读中的障碍,全面、深入、高效地阅读世界名著。

ABOUT THE AUTHOR

Born in Bombay (now Mumbai), India, on December 30, 1865, Rudyard Kipling made a significant contribution to English Literature covering all its three fields, poetry, short story and the novel.

His family was affluent, with his father an arts and crafts teacher at the Jeejeebhoy School of Art. His mother was the sister-in-law of the painter Edward Burne Jones.

He spent his early childhood in India, where an ayah took care of him. Under her influence he came in direct contact with the Indian culture and tradition. India at that time was ruled by the British.

At the age of six he was sent to a foster home in South sea. He records his unhappy life there in the novel *The Light That Failed,* and in his autobiography.

His poor eyesight and mediocre results ended his hopes of a military career. Kipling returned to India and worked as a journal-

关 于 作 者

罗德亚德·吉卜林于1865年12月30日出生在如今印度的孟买。他在诗歌、短篇故事和小说3个方面对英国文学做出了杰出贡献。

他家境富裕,父亲是吉吉卜浩艺术学校的手工艺学科教员,母亲则是画家埃德华·伯恩·琼斯的妻妹。

他幼年时期在印度度过,那里一个保姆照顾他的起居。在她的影响下,他同印度传统和印度文化进行了直接的接触。当时的印度由英国管辖。

6岁时,他被送往南部海岸的一户家庭寄养。他在小说《消失的光芒》和自传中记录了那段不幸的生活。

由于视力不佳和成绩不理想,他梦想从戎的希望落空了。他返回印度,于1882至1887年间在拉合尔当记者。之后的1887年至

ist in Lahore from 1882 to 1887. Then he worked as an overseas correspondent in Allahabad for the *Pioneer* from 1887 to 1889.

Two years later he published his collection of short stories *The Phantom Rickshaw*. In 1891 came a collection of Indian short stories *Life's Handicap*. His *Bareack Room Ballads'* became very popular, and included *Gunga Din*.

Kipling's marriage was not successful and in these restless years he wrote, many inventions, *Jungle Book, The Second Jungle Book* and *The Seven Seas*.

Widely regarded as the unofficial Poet Laureate, Kipling refused this and many other honours. In 1902 he moved to Sussex and was given a house by Cecil Rhodes, the influential British colonial statesman.

Kim appeared in 1901 and was widely acclaimed Kipling's best novel. In 1907, he received the Nobel Prize in Literature in consideration of the power of observation, originality of ideas, and a remarkable talent of narration.

The death of both his children, Josephine and John, deeply affected his life. As he grew older, his works showed the strain, mental and physical agony.

He died in 1936, leaving behind a legacy that will last for centuries to come.

1889 年间，他担任了《先锋报》在阿拉哈巴德的海外记者。

两年以后，他出版了短篇小说集《人力车幻影》。1891 年印度短篇小说集《生命的阻力》问世。他的《军营歌谣》很受欢迎，其中就包括《甘加丁》一诗。

吉卜林的婚姻不成功，在这些年中他笔耕不辍，写了许多作品，如《丛林故事》、《丛林故事续篇》和《七海》。

尽管吉卜林被广泛认为是非官方的"桂冠诗人"，可他拒绝了除此以外还有的其他许多荣誉。1902 年一位很有影响力的英国殖民地官员西塞尔·罗德斯给他提供了一处寓所，他便移居到了萨塞克斯。

《吉姆》于 1901 年出版，被普遍认为是吉卜林最好的一部小说。1907 年，吉卜林因为他的观察力、原创思想和出色的描写才能而被授予诺贝尔文学奖。

他的两个孩子——约瑟芬和约翰的死亡，极大地影响了他的生活。随着年龄的增长，他的作品显示出压力、精神和肉体的痛苦挣扎。

他于 1936 年辞世，他留下的遗产将会在将来的若干个世纪中延续。

CONTENTS

目 录

1

KIM'S PARENTAGE AND THE LAMA FROM TIBET

He sat, in defiance of municipal orders, *astride*[1] the gun Zam-Zammah, opposite the old Ajaib Ghar — the Wonder House, as the natives called the Lahore Museum.

Though he was burned black as any native; though he spoke the vernacular by *preference*, and his mother tongue in a certain singsong way; though he behaved with terms of perfect equality with small boys of the bazaar; Kim was white. His mother had been nursemaid in a Colonel's family and had married Kimball O'Hara, a young sergeant of the Mavericks, an Irish regiment. He afterwards took a post in Punjab, and Delhi Railway, and his Regiment went home without him. His wife died of cholera in Ferozepore, and O'Hara fell to drink and loafing with a keen-eyed three-year old baby.

Societies and chaplains, anxious for the child, tried to catch

---

1.本书正文中的斜体英文在文末词汇表中均有注释。——编者注

一

吉姆的身世和
来自西藏的喇嘛

他无视政府的三令五申，跨坐在参参玛大炮上。这尊大炮对面是历史悠久的阿杰布格尔——珍奇馆的意思，当地人叫它拉合尔博物馆。

虽然他同当地人一样皮肤晒得黝黑；虽然他喜欢讲土话，说起母语来声音单调；虽然他跟街市上那些小男孩完全平等相处，但吉姆是白种人。他的母亲在上校家当过保姆并嫁给了爱尔兰小牛团的年轻中士吉姆波尔·欧哈拉。吉姆波尔后来在旁遮普和德里铁路上做过事，他那个团回国时他没有跟着回去。欧哈拉的老婆在费罗兹普尔死于霍乱，这以后欧哈拉便开始酗酒，成天带着他那目光锐利的三岁男孩闲逛。

一些社团和随军牧师放心不下那孩子，想尽力抓住他，

him, but O'Hara drifted away, till he came across a woman
who took opium. He learned the taste from her, and died a
poor man. At his death he left his son nothing, except his
birth certificate, which he said would make young Kimball a
man.

Under the effect of opium, he would say that all would
come right some day. The Colonel himself, riding on a horse,
at the head of the finest Regiment in the world, would attend
to Kim — little Kim that should have been better than his
father. Nine hundred first-class devils, whose God was a Red
Bull on a green field, would attend to Kim — only if they
had not forgotten O' Hara. Then he would weep bitterly.

So it came about that after his death the Indian woman
sewed the birth certificate into a small leather case, which
she strung round Kim's neck. She would confusedly repeat
colonel O'Hara's words, all in the wrong order.

"Ah," said Kim, "I shall remember. A Red Bull and a Colonel on a horse would come, but first, my father said, will
come two men making ready the ground for these matters.
That is how my father said they always did; and it is always
so when men work magic."

Kim held views of his own. As he reached an age where
he could understand, he learned to avoid white men and
missionaries. True, he did nothing with great success.

可是欧哈拉总是能溜走。直到后来他遇上一个抽鸦片的女人，并从她那里染上了抽鸦片的嗜好，随后就穷困潦倒地去世了。除了吉姆的出生证明，他什么也没留下。他说，这一样东西会使小吉姆成为一个真正的男人。

在鸦片的作用下，他会说，总有一天，一切都会好起来的，骑着骏马、率领着世上最精锐的军队的那个上校会亲自来伺候吉姆，小吉姆的日子本来就该过得比父亲好。九百个奉草原大红牛为神的一流小精灵也会来伺候吉姆，只要他们没忘了欧哈拉。说完这些，他便会痛哭一阵。

因此，他死后，那女人就将那份出生证明缝在一个小皮囊里，挂在吉姆的脖子上。她总是颠三倒四地回忆着欧哈拉的预言。

"呃，"吉姆说，"我会记住的。一头红牛还有一个骑马的上校会来。不过，父亲说了，先会有两个人来做准备。父亲说了，人家都是这样做的，人家施魔法时都是这样的。"

吉姆有他自己的想法，当他到了能够了解的年龄时，他学会了避开传教士和白人。确实，吉姆还未成就什么大事。

He sat on the Zam-Zammah, and drummed his heels against it.

Kim suddenly stopped, for those shuffled round the corner, a man, such as Kim had never seen. He was nearby six feet high, dressed in fold upon fold of stuff like horse-blanketing. At his belt hung a long iron pen case and a wooden *rosary* such as holy men wear. On his head was a huge wide hat, and his face yellow and wrinkled like the Chinese bootman.

"Who is that?" said Kim to his companions.

"Perhaps it is a man," said Abdullah, staring.

"A priest, perhaps," said Chotalal, noticing his rosary.

"O! Children, what is that big house?" He asked in fair Urdu.

"The Ajaib Ghar, the Wonder House!" said Kim, not being able to understand the man's creed, and asked, "What is your caste? Where is your house? Have you come from far?"

"I came by Kulu — from beyond Kailash — from the hills, where the air and water are fresh and cool. Aye, child. I am a Tibetan. Have you heard of Tibet? I am a Lama — or, say, a guru in your tongue."

"A guru from Tibet," said Kim, "I have not seen such a man. Are there Hindus in Tibet, then?"

"We are followers of the Middle Way," he said, "a living in peace. Now I go to see the Four Holy Places before I die. Are there many images in the Wonder House of Lahore?"

"Yes, it is true," said Kim, "Come with me and I'll show you."

他骑在参参玛大炮上，还一边用脚后跟敲打着它。

忽然，他停住了，因为从喧闹的拐角处走过来一个人——一个他从没见过的人。他身高近六英尺，穿着一件像马毯子一样皱巴巴的衣服。他的腰带上挂着一个长长的铁制笔盒，还有一串僧侣戴的木念珠，头戴一顶大扁圆帽。他脸呈黄色，布满皱纹，跟中国鞋匠一样。

"那人是谁？"吉姆问伙伴们。

"可能是个男人。"阿卜杜拉眼盯着那人说。

"也许是个和尚吧。"乔塔·拉尔发现了那串念珠。

"嘿，孩子们，那大房子是做什么用的？"他用还算过得去的乌尔都语问道。

"那是阿杰布格尔，珍奇馆！"吉姆说，因为猜不出那人信什么教，又问道，"你是什么种姓？你家在哪？你从很远的地方来吗？"

"我从库鲁——就是凯拉斯还要过去的山里来，那里的空气和水又新鲜又清凉。哎，孩子，我是西藏人，你们听说过西藏吗？我是个喇嘛，或者，用你们的话说叫法师。"

"西藏法师，"吉姆说，"我从没见过这样的人。那他们是西藏的印度人喽？"

"我们是中道宗教信徒，与世无争。我要在死之前去看看四大圣地。拉合尔珍奇馆里真的有很多佛像吗？"

"是的，"吉姆说，"跟我来，我带你去看看。"

The old man followed Kim, and halted amazed at the entrance of the Hall.

In open-mouthed wonder, the Lama stood at this and that, and finally stood before a large statue of Lord Buddha.

"The Lord! The Lord! It is the Sakya Muni himself, and he is here. My pilgrimage is well-begun. What work ! What work!"

"Yonder is the Sahib," said Kim, pointing to the *curator* of the museum, who was a white-bearded Englishman, and was looking at the Lama. The priest from Tibet *gravely* turned and saluted him, and drew forth a notebook and a piece of paper.

"Yes, that is my name," and the Englishman smiled at the clumsy, childish handwriting.

"The Lama of Lung Cho Monastery gave it to me," said the lama, "he spoke of these," and he pointed to the statues around with a thin and trembling hand.

"Welcome, then, O Lama from Tibet. Here are the images for you to see, and I am here to gather knowledge from you. Come to my office awhile."

The office was a small wooden cabin, partitioned off from the gallery. Kim laid himself down, his ear against a crack, and following his instinct, stretched out to listen and watch.

老人跟着吉姆，刚进门口就停住了，不胜惊讶。

喇嘛看得目瞪口呆，转过来转过去，最后停在一件巨大的佛像前。

"世尊！世尊！这是释迦牟尼真身，我的朝圣之行旗开得胜。真是巧夺天工！巧夺天工啊！"

"洋大人在那边，"吉姆说时，指着博物馆的馆长，那是一个胡子花白的英国人，他正看着喇嘛，喇嘛神情庄重地转过身来，向他点头致意，然后掏出一个笔记本和一张纸片。

"这是我的名字。"英国人看着拙劣、稚气的字体笑了。

"这是龙珠寺的喇嘛给我的，"喇嘛说，"他说过这些的。"他颤抖着瘦瘦的手指指点点。

"欢迎，欢迎啊，西藏来的喇嘛。这里有您想看的佛像，我在这里可以向您求知识。请到我的办公室坐一会儿。"

办公室是用木板在陈列室里隔出的一个小单间。吉姆躺了下来，耳朵贴在缝隙上，本能驱使他倾听并观察里面的动静。

Most of the talk went above his head. The Lama spoke to the curator about his own lammasery, and the curator brought out a book and showed him that very place.

"You English know of these things? The Lord has honour here too? And his life is known?"

"It is all carved upon the stones. Come and see."

The two men shuffled out to the main hall, and went through the whole collection with *reverence* and appreciation.

Incident by incident the beautiful story was identified on the stone. The curator soon saw that his guest was no ordinary bead-telling priest, but a scholar, who spoke a mixture of Urdu and Tibetan.

He had heard of the travels of Fa-Hien and Huen-Tsang, and was anxious to know if there was any translation of their records. For the first time he came to know how the European scholars had laboured to identify the holy places of buddhism.

The Lama lowered his voice. "And I come here alone. I go to free myself from the Wheel of Things. As a pilgrim to the holy places I acquire merit. But there is one more thing. When our gracious Lord was but a youth, when his marriage was sought, the people said he was too tender for marriage. Did you know this?"

大部分的谈话他根本听不懂。喇嘛讲起了他的喇嘛寺。馆长拿出了一本书,让他看那个地方。

"你们英国人也知道这些事吗?世尊在这里也受尊崇吗?他的生平这里的人也知道?"

"全都刻在石头上呢!过来看看。"

二人步履蹒跚地走进大厅,怀着虔诚和欣赏逐个观看藏品。

石头上依稀可辨一个个美妙动人的故事。馆长马上便看出他的客人不是个只会手掐念珠喃喃有词的僧人,而是一个极富才华的学者,混合讲着乌尔都语和藏语。

他听说过高僧法显和玄奘写的印度取经记,很想知道有没有译本。他第一次听说欧洲学者们是怎样地付出劳动鉴定出各佛教圣地。

喇嘛放低声音说:"我只身一人来到这里,我要摆脱轮回。要去各地朝觐以积功德。不过远不止这点。我佛如来少年求婚配时,有人说他年龄太小,不宜结婚。这事你知道吗?"

The curator nodded.

"So they made a trial of strength against all comers. The test was of the bow, and our Lord broke the first one which they gave him. Then he called for one that could not be broken. Did you know this?"

The Englishman said, "I have read this."

"The Lord overshot all other marks, and the arrow passed far and beyond sight. At last it fell. Where it touched the earth, there broke out a stream, which became a river, which had the merits of its creator. He who bathes in it washes away all sin."The curator nodded.

"The surely you must know. I beg you, I am an old man. We know he drew the bow! We know the arrow fell! We know the stream gushed! Where then is the river? My dream told me to find it — The River of Arrow! I am sure no one would cheat an old man."

"I do not know. I do not know."

The Lama brought his thousand-wrinkled face very close to the curator's face. "I see you do not know. But I am bound to go. Will you cóme with me?"

馆长点点头。

"因此他们请佛陀与所有来者进行较力测验。测验射箭时，佛陀把他们给他的箭弓拉断了，然后又叫人拿来一具没有人拉得动的弓。这事你知道吗？"

"我看过。"英国人说。

"他射出的那只箭飞过所有的靶子，飞往远远超过眼力能及的地方。最后箭落下来了，落下的地方便涌出一条小溪，转眼就变成河流。因为世尊慈悲为怀，谁在那条河里沐浴，谁就可以涤瑕荡垢，冲洗罪孽。"馆长点头。

"你一定知道吧？我求你了！我是个老人，我们知道他拉满弓！我们知道那支箭落下！我们知道泉水涌现！可是那条河在哪里呢？我的梦让我要找到它。那条箭河！我相信没人会欺骗一个老人的。"

"我不知道，我真的不知道。"

喇嘛再次把那张布满皱纹的脸凑近英国人的脸："我看出你是真的不知道。可我一定得去，你愿意和我一起去吗？"

2

THE LAMA'S QUEST

"**B**ut where will you go?" asked the curator.
"First I shall go to Kashi (Benaras), where I will meet
a pure follower of the Jain Faith. May be he will go with me.
I will go everywhere as I go — for the place where the arrow
fell is not known."

"But how will you go?" asked the curator.

"By roads mainly. Trains cramp me, and I am used to
walking. I will follow the places of His life till I come to The
River of Arrow."

"And for food?"

"For the journey, I take up the Master's begging bowl. I
have no disciples now, so I will take up the alms-bowl."

The Lama nodded valiantly. He was an enthusiast in his
quest.

"Let me now gain some merit. Here is a new book of white
English Paper, and here are some sharpened pencils — thick and
thin," said the curator, and added, "now lend me thy spectacles."

二

喇嘛的要求

"不过你要去哪里呢？"

"先到克什（贝纳勒斯），我要去见一位净土宗派人士，或许他会和我一块儿去。我要一路找过去，因为箭到底落在哪里还没有人知道。"

"可是你怎么去？"馆长问。

"主要是走着去。火车会挤得我很难受，我是习惯走路的。我要沿着世尊生前的足迹，一直走到箭河。"

"那么吃的呢？"

"一路上我都会用世尊的乞钵。现在我身边没有弟子，所以我要自己拿着乞钵化缘。"

他点点头，一副无所畏惧的神态，他乐于做这事。

"请允许我现在就积点功德。这里有一本新的英国白纸簿，几支削好的铅笔——有粗有细，"馆长接着又说，"现在把你的眼镜借给我戴戴。"

The curator looked through them. They were heavily scratched, but the power was almost as his own pair. He slid it into the lama's hand saying, "Try these."

The old man tried them, and turned his head delightedly. "I scarcely feel them! How clearly do I see!"

"They will never scratch. Maybe they help you to find your River. You can keep them."

"I will take them as a sign of friendship between priest and priest — and now — " the Lama fumbled at his belt, and took out an open-work iron pen case, and laid it at the Curator's table.

"That is for a memory between you and me — my pen case is something as old — as I am."

The pen case was of ancient Chinese design, not available now.

"When I return, having found the River, I will bring you a written picture of the Padma Samthora — as I used to make on silk at the monastery — and also the Wheel of Life."

The Buddhist was a conventional brush-pen artist — and not many were left now. The curator saw the Lama stride out, head in air, pausing in meditation at the great statue of the Bodhisat.

Kim followed him like a shadow. What he had overheard

　　馆长戴上眼镜看出去。镜片上有许多刮痕，但是光度几乎和他自己那副完全一样，他把自己的眼镜塞到喇嘛手里："试试这副。"

　　老人试着戴上了它，高兴得头直晃："我几乎感觉不到它的存在，我看得多清楚啊！"

　　"它们永远不会有刮痕，也许它能帮你找到那条河。它就是你的了。"

　　"我都收下了，"喇嘛说，"作为修行人之间的友谊象征——现在——"他在腰带上摸索，解下那个铁制无盖笔盒，放在馆长的桌子上。

　　"把这个笔盒当做纪念物——纪念你我之间这段缘分。这是件古董，和我的年纪一般大呢。"

　　这个笔盒是古代的设计，中国款式，如今已经没有了。

　　"等我找到那条河回来时，会给你一幅写画，像我以前在喇嘛寺里写画在丝绸布上的那种莲花妙轮。还有轮回图。"

　　这佛教徒是这世上屈指可数的身怀佛教传统写画笔技的人。喇嘛昂首阔步往外走去，在一尊静坐默想的佛像前驻足片刻。

　　吉姆像个影子跟在后面。他在旁边听到的一切令他激动

excited him wildly. The man was entirely new to his experience, and he meant to investigate further.

The Lama halted by the zam-zammah, and looked round till his eyes fell on Kim. He looked so old and lovely that Kim felt sympathy for the Lama.

"What do you do?"

"I beg. It is long since I have eaten or drunk. What is the custom of begging in this town? In silence or begging aloud?"

"Those who beg in silence, starve in silence," said Kim, "Give me the bowl, I know the people of this city — they are all charitable. I will bring it back filled."

Simply as a child, the old man handed Kim the bowl.

"Rest now," said Kim, and trotted off.Soon he was back with a bowl full of hot rice, steaming vegetable curry, with ghee, a fried cake and a lump of tamarind preserve.

The Lama's eyes opened wide at seeing the contents of the bowl."Eat now — and I will eat with thee."

They ate together in great content, and cleared the begging bowl. Then the Lama fingered his rosary a while, and dropped into the easy sleep of age under the shadow of the zam-zammah.

不已。他从没见过像喇嘛这样的人，他要进一步探究他。

老喇嘛在参参玛大炮前停下，朝四周看看，最后，目光落在吉姆身上。他看起来如此老迈、无辜，使吉姆对他的同情心油然而生。

"你是做什么的？"

"我行乞。我已经很久没吃没喝了。这个城里求人布施有什么风俗吗？是默不作声还是出声求食呢？"

"默默行乞就得默默挨饿，"吉姆回答，"把钵给我，我认识这个城里的人，他们都很好心，我会把它装满了拿回来。"

老喇嘛像个孩子似的把钵给了吉姆。

"你歇一歇。"吉姆说着便跑掉了。他很快就回来了，钵里有热气腾腾的饭和蔬菜咖喱，上面还有一块炸糕和一小堆酸罗望子蜜饯。

看着钵里的饭菜，喇嘛的眼睛睁得老大。"吃吧，我和你一起吃。"

他们俩心满意足地一起吃了起来，把钵里的东西吃了个精光。吃完饭后，喇嘛掐了一会儿念珠，一眨眼的工夫便在参参玛大炮的影子里睡着了。

The Lama did not wake up till the evening life of the city had begun with lamp-lighting. While the Lama had slept Kim had run away to change his western attire of shirt and trousers for a set of Hindu dress.

So when the Lama woke up and looked around for Kim, he did not find him. Only a Hindu street boy in a dirty turban was there. The Lama wailed in sorrow, his head on his knees.

"What is this?" said the boy before him. "Have you been robbed?"

"It is my new chela (disciple). He has gone away from me, and I don't know where he is. He led me to the Wonder House, and gave me strength to speak to the curator of the museum. And when I was weak with hunger, he begged for me, as a chela for his teacher. Suddenly, he has gone away. It was in my mind to have taught him the law upon the road to Benaras."

Kim stood amazed. He knew the man spoke the truth for he had overheard their talk.

"I know he was sent for a purpose — to find a certain river I seek."

"The River of Arrow?" Kim said with a knowing smile.

"To none have I spoken of my search, save the priest of the images. Who art thou?"

"Your chela," said Kim, "I have never seen anyone like

喇嘛一觉醒来，已是华灯初上，夜生活开始了。在喇嘛睡觉时，吉姆跑开了，把他本来的衣服换下，穿上了一身印度装。

所以当喇嘛醒来时，四下张望，除了一个头缠肮脏头巾的印度孩子，什么也没有。他把头埋到膝盖上，低声哭泣起来。

"怎么啦？"那孩子站在他面前问道，"你被人抢了吗？"

"是我的新弟子，他弃我而去了，我不知道他在哪里。他带我走进那珍奇馆，让我鼓起勇气和那管佛像的人讲话。我饿得快晕倒时，他替我去乞食，就像弟子服侍师父那样，他突然离我而去。我本想在去贝纳勒斯的路上，把大法传授给他的。"

吉姆在一旁怔住了，因为他已经听到了博物馆里的谈话，他知道老喇嘛讲的是真话。

"我现在明白他是受命而来——让我知道自己能找到要找的那条河。"
"是箭河吗？"吉姆问道，脸上露出早就知道的神情。
"除了那个管神像的番僧，我可没跟别人讲起我在寻找什么。你是谁呢？"
"你的弟子，"吉姆回答，"我长这么大还没见过像你这

you in all my life. I will go with you to Benaras. I heard when you were speaking to the Englishman.

"You don't know the River, then?" said the Lama.

"No," Kim laughed uneasily. "I go to look for — for a bull — a red bull on a green field who will help me. So my father told me. If it is our fate to find those things we shall find them — you, your River, and I, my Bull."

"Come, let us go to Benaras," said the Lama.

"Now by night," said Kim. " Thieves are around. Wait till the day!"

"But there is no place to sleep," said the Lama.

"We shall get lodging at the Kashmir Serai," said Kim,"I have a friend there. Come!"

样的人。我跟你到贝纳勒斯去。那是你在跟那英国人讲话时我听到的。"

"这么说，你并不知道箭河在哪里喽？"喇嘛说。

"我不知道，"吉姆不自在地笑着说，"我是去找草原上的一头公牛，它会帮我的。我父亲是这么跟我说的。要是我们命中注定要找到那些东西，我们就会找到——你找到你的河；我呢，找到我的牛。"

"我们到贝纳勒斯去吧。"喇嘛说。

"晚上不能走，"吉姆说，"到处都是盗贼。得等天亮再走！"

"但那没地方住。"喇嘛说。

"我们在喀什米尔客栈投宿。"吉姆说，"我在那里有朋友。走吧！"

3

MAHBUB ALI AT THE KASHMIR SERAI

Kim guided the Lama through to Mahbub Ali, the horse-trader. He had many dealings with Mahbub Ali in his little life. Sometimes he would tell Kim to keep watch on a man, or follow him through the days and report all whom he talked to. It was some kind of secret plot, Kim knew, but he spoke to no one about it, for Mahbub gave him delicious meals, and once he got eight annas (equal to fifty paise) in money.

When Kim brought in the lama, Mabhub Ali was lying on a silk carpet, enjoying a silver hookah.

"Allah! A Lama! A red Lama! It is far from Tibet to Lahore. What are you doing here?"

The trader gave no sign of astonishment, but looked at Kim from under his bushy eyebrows.

三

喀什米尔客栈的
马哈布·阿里

吉姆领着喇嘛，穿过人群，到了马贩阿里的地方。在吉姆还小的时候，就已经和马哈布打过多次交道。有时他会叫吉姆盯梢一个人，跟踪他一天，然后向马哈布一一汇报这个人都和哪些人说过话。吉姆知道这是某种阴谋勾当，不过，他对任何人都守口如瓶，为此，马哈布请他吃过美餐，有一回，还给他多达八安纳的钱。

当吉姆把喇嘛带进房间时，马贩子正躺在一副丝毯鞍囊上，抽着一个银制的大水烟筒。

"真主啊！是个喇嘛！一个红教喇嘛！从西藏到拉合尔够远的。你来这儿干什么？"

马贩子并没有露出惊讶的神色，而是用浓眉下的双眼注视着吉姆。

"Little friend of the World," said he, "what is this?"

"Nothing. I am now the holy man's disciple, and we are going on a pilgrimage together to Benaras."

"But why come to me?" asked the trader suspiciously.

"To whom should I go? I have no money. You will sell many horses. Give me a rupee, when I come into wealth, I'll repay it."

"You have never lied to me before," said Mahbub Ali, thinking swiftly. "Call that Lama — stand back in the dark."

"Our tales will agree," said Kim.

"We go to Benaras," said the Lama, as soon as he understood Mahbub Ali's question, "the boy and I go — I go to seek a certain river."

"And the boy?"

"He was sent, I think, to guide me the river."

"His name?"

"That I did not ask. He is my disciple. Will anyone take him from me? Without him, I shall not find my river."

"No one will take him from you," said Mahbub Ali. The Lama returned to the hill man, and Kim came forward.

"Why should I lie to you Hajji?"

Mahbub puffed his hookah in silence, but lost in thought. Then he spoke almost in a whisper. "Umballa (Ambala) is on the road to Benares — if indeed you are going there. Will you carry a message for me? I will give you money."

"小朋友，"他说，"你这是搞什么名堂？"

"没什么。我现在是那个圣者的徒弟，我们一起去朝圣，到贝纳勒斯去。"

"为什么来找我？"马哈布疑惑地问道。

"我还能去找谁呢？我没钱。你要把好多马卖给军官。给我一个卢比吧，等我发财了，我保证会还给你的。"

马哈布考虑着："你以前从没对我撒过谎。把那个喇嘛叫过来，你退后站到暗处去。"

"我们说的会是一回事。"吉姆笑着说。

"我们要到贝纳勒斯去，"喇嘛一弄明白马哈布·阿里问话的意思就说，"这孩子和我。我去找一条河。"

"那男孩是……？"

"我想他是上天派来带我到那条河去的。"

"他叫什么名字呢？"

"我没问。他就是我的徒弟。难道有人想要把他从我身边抢走吗？没有他我就找不到我要找的那条河。"

"没有人会把他从你身边抢走的。"马哈布·阿里说道。喇嘛回到原来的位置，吉姆走上前来。

"我干吗要骗你呢，哈吉①？"

马哈布一声不吭抽着水烟沉思着，然后近乎耳语般地开口了："去贝纳勒斯得经过乌姆巴拉，你要是肯替我带个信到那儿，我就给你钱。"

---

①哈吉：过去对麦加朝圣者的尊称。

"Come nearer, and hold up hands as begging," said Mahbub Ali. "It concerns a horse — a white *stallion*. The *pedigree* of the horse was not fully established, and the officer in Umballa, bade me make it clear."

Mahbub described the house and the appearance of the officer. "So your message will be, 'the pedigree of the white stallion is fully established.' By this he will know you are coming from me. He will then ask you. 'What proof have you?' and you will answer. 'Mahbub Ali has given me the proof.'"

Kim giggled, his eyes shining, "and all for a white stallion?"

"That pedigree I will give you now, in my own way, and some hard words as well."

A shadow passed behind Kim and Mahbub raised his voice. "Go, and lie down among horse-boys tonight — you and the Lama."

Kim shrank away, and as expected, he found a small wad of folded tissue paper wrapped in oilskin, and three silver rupees. He smiled and thrust the paper and the money into his leather *amulet* case.

The Lama had fed well and was already asleep. Kim lay down beside him. He knew he had done Mahbub Ali a service. Not for one minute did he believe the story of the pedigree.

"站过来靠近些，伸出手来像要饭的样子，这是有关于一匹马—— 一匹白色的公马，马的血统还没有完全确定，那个军官让我查清楚，他人就在乌姆巴拉。"

马哈布描述了那匹马和那个军官的长相。"口信就说，'那匹白种马的血统已经完全确定。'这么一说，他便会明白你是我派去的。然后他会问，'你有什么证据？'你就回答，'马哈布·阿里已经把证据给我了。'"

"就为一匹白种马？"吉姆笑着说道，两眼闪闪发光。

"那张血统证明我现在就给你——用我自己的独特方式给你——不过还得讲些难听的话。"

一个影子从吉姆身后掠过，马哈布提高嗓门："去和我的马夫过夜——你和那个喇嘛。"

吉姆溜开了。不出所料，他发现油布里包着一个卫生纸折叠成的小纸团，里面有三个卢比。他微微一笑，把钱和纸一起塞进挂在脖子上的避邪皮囊里。

喇嘛饱餐一顿，已经睡着了。吉姆在他身边躺下。他知道自己帮了马哈布·阿里的忙，他根本不信什么白种马血统证明的鬼话。

But Kim did not suspect that Mahbub Ali, one of the best horse dealers, was registered with the government as c.25. IB. Twice or thrice yearly, c.25 would send in a little story about mountain kingdoms, gun trade, and foreigners visiting India.

Now, Mahbub Ali had this important wad of closely folded tissue paper, with five microscopic pin holes. It gave information about a Northern Power, a Hindu banker in Peshawar, a firm of gun makers in Belgium and an important semi-independent Mohammedan ruler in South. The last was R.17's work.It was not safe for him to leave his post, and the sooner the information reached proper hands, the better. A wandering Lama with a low caste boy servant might attract attention and interest, but no one would suspect them, or even rob them.

Then Mahbub Ali went across the Serai on a visit, where a girl searched him thoroughly.

About the same time, Kim heard a man come to Mahbub's room, and went through every single box, handle, mat, and saddlebag, and found nothing.

"I think he is only an Afghan horse dealer. This is not the man."

Kim had watched secretly the man's searching, and knew this was no common thief. His knife had slit slippers and saddlebags.

吉姆怎么会知道,这个最棒的马贩之一在政府中注册的代号是 C.25.IB。每年 C.25 都会递交两三次小报告。都是关于外国人访问印度啦,枪支买卖的事情。

现在这重要的东西就在马哈布身上,这是一个折了好几折的卫生纸纸团,上面有五个小孔,它们令人震惊地出卖了五个结盟藩王、北方的同情势力、白沙瓦的一个印度银行家、比利时的一家枪炮制造公司和南方一个地位显赫的半独立的穆斯林统治者。这个密件是 R.17 的杰作。R.17 不能离开他的监视岗位。这个密件越早送到合适的人手里越好。一个喇嘛带着一个低种姓童仆云游,也许会吸引人们片刻的兴趣,但是没有人会怀疑他们,更没有人会去抢劫他们。

马哈布摇摇晃晃地走出客栈,那里的妓女几乎把他从头到脚仔仔细细搜了一遍。

几乎在这同时,吉姆听到马哈布的房间里有轻轻的脚步声。每一只箱子,每一捆包裹,每一张席子,每一副鞍囊,都被翻查了一遍,可一无所获。

"依我看,他只不过是个马贩子而已,不是我们要找的那个人。"

吉姆偷偷地看着他们在那边搜查,知道他们并不是一般的小偷。他的小刀划开了拖鞋后跟,挑断了鞍囊的缝线。

"It must be the thing I carry to Umballa with me. Better we go now. Those who search bags with knives, may search bellies with knives."

So he had wakened the Lama and said,"Come. It is time to go to Benaras."

The Lama rose obediently, and they passed out of the serai like shadows.

When Mahbub Ali returned, he found his men asleep, but there was no sign of the Lama and the boy.

Kim stole out, and following Mahbub Ali's directions, easily found the house of the Englishman. Kim slipped through the garden hedge and hid behind some tall grass. The house was brightly lit, and servants moved about tables, arranged with flowers, glass and silver. Soon an Englishman came out, humming a tune. It was too dark to see his face, so Kim tried his beggar trick.

"Protector of the Poor!"
The man backed towards the voice.
"Mahabub Ali says — "
"Hah! What says Mahbub Ali?" He made no attempt to look for the speaker, that showed Kim that he knew.
"The pedigree of the white stallion is fully established."
"What proof is there?" The Englishman turned to the hedge.

"那肯定是我要带到乌姆巴拉去的东西。我们最好现在就走。那些用刀搜查包袱的人说不定还会动刀子呢。"

所以他叫醒了喇嘛说："走吧,该是去贝纳勒斯的时候了。"

喇嘛顺从地起来,他们像幽灵一样溜出了客栈。

当马哈布回来时,他发现自己的随从呼呼大睡,男孩和喇嘛却无影无踪。

吉姆溜出来后,按照马哈布的指点,轻轻松松就找到了英国人的房子。他从花园篱笆钻进去,躲在高大的树丛后。屋内灯火通明,仆人们在摆着鲜花、酒杯和银餐具的桌子间忙碌。不一会儿,有个英国人走出来,哼着曲子。天色太黑,看不清他的脸,吉姆尝试着用乞丐的小伎俩。

"穷人的保护神!"
那人转过身来朝着发出声音的方向。
"马哈布·阿里说——"
"噢,马哈布·阿里说什么了?"他并没有试图寻找说话的人,凭这点吉姆明白他知道这件事。
"那匹白种马的血统已经完全确定。"
"你有什么证据?"英国人转身朝着篱笆。

"Mahbub Ali has given me this proof!" Kim flipped the wad of folded paper into the air, and it fell on the path beside the man, who put his foot on it as the gardener came round the corner. When the servant had passed he picked it up, and left a rupee on the ground, and strode into the house without looking back.

Swiftly Kim took up the money, but desiring to know the effect of his action, lay close in the grass and crept nearer to the house.

Indian bungalows are very open. He could see the Englishman return to a small dressing room, and sit down to study Mahbub Ali's message by a kerosene lamp. Kim noted his face change and darken.

The man dashed out bare-headed and met a tall black-haired man and a young officer. His Englishman and the black stranger exchanged two sentences.

"We shan't be twenty minutes," said Kim's man, and with the black-haired man, came back to the dressing room. Kim saw their heads bent over Mahbub Ali's message.

Kim heard, "I had been expecting this — Mahbub Ali's paper confirms it. Grogan's dining here tonight, isn't he?"

"Yes sir, and Macklin too."

"马哈布·阿里已经把证据给我了。"吉姆往空中抛出那个纸团，纸团落在那人身旁的小径上，他一脚踩住，因为有个花匠正拐过屋角走过来。花匠过去后，他捡起纸团，丢下一个卢比，头也不回大踏步走进屋里。

吉姆敏捷地拾起钱来，可是他很想知道此次行动的效果，于是他紧贴着草地，匍匐到房子近旁。

印度式的平房无遮无挡。他看到那个英国人回到了一间小梳妆室，坐了下来，在煤油灯下开始研究马哈布·阿里的密件。吉姆注意到他的脸色变了，表情阴沉。

那人没戴帽子就冲了出去，他遇到了一个黑发的高个和一个年轻的军官。那英国人和黑发的陌生人交谈了两句。

"我们不会超过二十分钟，"那英国人说，然后和那黑发的人回到了梳妆室。吉姆看到他们埋头细读马哈布·阿里的密件。

吉姆听到他们说："我早就料到要这么办，马哈布·阿里的密件证实了这种猜测。戈罗甘今晚在这里吃饭了，是不是？"

"是的，长官，还有麦克林。"

"Very good. I'll speak to them myself. Warn Pindi and Peshawar brigades. Eight thousand should be enough."

"Then it means war?"

"No. Punishment," and they walked out.

Kim crawled round to the back of the house for food — and information. The kitchen was crowded with servants, one of them kicked him.

"Aie," said Kim, "I only came to wash dishes in return for food."

"Get hence. We who serve Creighton Sahib do not need strangers to help us through a big dinner."

"It is a very big dinner," said Kim looking at the plates.

"No wonder. The guest of honour is the Jangi Lat Sahib — the Commander in Chief of the Army."

"Ho!" said Kim with a note of wonder. He had learned what he had wanted, and when the servant looked again, he was gone.

"Wish I had crept nearer," thought Kim. "It is a big news."

“很好，我会亲自跟他们说。通知品第和白沙瓦各派，八千人应该足够了。”

“那么说就是要开战了？”

“不，是惩罚。”然后他们走了出来。

吉姆匍匐着绕到房子后面找食物还有打听消息。厨房里挤满了仆人，其中一个踢了他一下。

“哎呦，”吉姆说，“我只是来洗洗盘子换填饱肚子的呀。”

“走开，我们这些服侍克莱顿大人的不需要生人来帮忙应付盛宴。”

“真是一场盛宴啊。”吉姆看着盘子说。

“没什么好奇怪的，今天的贵宾可是总司令大人哪。”

“哦，”吉姆惊讶地叫了一声。他已经刺探到了他想知道的事。当仆人再看时，他已经溜走了。

“要是那时爬得更近些就好了，”吉姆想着，“这可是大新闻哪！”

4

THE JOURNEY BY ROAD

The two walked on, the Lama answering all questions with simplicity. They sought a river — a river of miraculous healing. Some laughed, but more offered them shade and meals.

A smooth-shaven priest told him, "The *virtue* of your River lies neither in one pool nor in one place, but throughout its length. If God wills it, be sure you will come upon your freedom."

"That is well said," the Lama was much impressed. "We will begin tomorrow."

The first freshness of the day carried the Lama forward with long, easy, camel-like strides. He was deep in meditation, clicking his rosary. They followed the worn country road, and saw all India at work in the fields.

The Grand Trunk Road was a wonderful spectacle. It ran straight, bearing India's traffic for fifteen miles — truly like a river of life as exists nowhere in the world.

四

沿途旅行

他们两个人走着，喇嘛始终简单地回答着所有的问题。他们在寻找一条河——一条能治病洗罪的奇妙的河。有人哈哈大笑，更多的人则请他们在树荫下坐一坐，再吃顿饭。

脸庞刮得光亮的村僧回答道："你那条河的神力不是在一处水潭或者一个地方，而是贯穿在整条河里。如果神有意的话，你就一定能够获得解脱。"

"说得在理。"喇嘛觉得这个主意很好。
"我们明天就动身吧。"

喇嘛呼吸着清新的空气，迈开从容、骆驼似的大步朝前走去。他潜神默思，同时手掐念珠。他们沿着坑坑洼洼的乡间土路行走。整个印度都在田野里忙碌着。

大干道十分壮观。道路笔直，担负着印度十五英里的交通运输，这样一条生命的河流在世界上是绝无仅有的。

The Lama remained deep in meditation, but Kim's eyes were wide open. This broad, smiling river of life was a vast improvement on the cramped and crowded Lahore streets. There were new people and new sights at every side.

The Lama never raised his eyes, and strode steadily hour after hour. His soul was busy elsewhere. But Kim was in the seventh heaven of joy, seeing India spread out to left and right. Kim felt these things, but could not give tongue to his feelings, and the Lama never spoke.

The crowd thickened as they neared the resting place. The sun was beginning to set, and the birds flew back home into their nests.

The life of the "parao"(resting place) was the same as the Kashmir Serai, but on a smaller scale. Kim dived into the happy Asiatic disorder. His wants were few, because the Lama had no *scruples* of caste and creed, so cooked food from the nearby stalls would serve.

Kim noticed a gaily ornamented family bullock cart, which was just drawing into the "parao". Eight men followed it, with two of them armed with rusty *sabres*, Half of them were thin-legged, grey-bearded Oriyas from the South. The other half were hill men. The mixture told its own tale, even if he had not heard the hot words between the two parties.

　　喇嘛跟往常一样，潜神默思，吉姆却睁大双眼，目光炯炯。这条宽阔的微笑着的生命河流，他心想，比起拉合尔那些又窄又挤的街道来可强多了。四周都是新面孔、新景象。

　　喇嘛一路上没有抬起头来。一个又一个小时的过程中，他的灵魂在别处忙碌着，脚步却稳固地朝前迈进。吉姆像登上天似的乐不可支，观赏着整个印度在左右两边伸展开来。看着这些，吉姆深有感受，却无法用语言表达出来。喇嘛没有说话。

　　他们走近歇脚处时，人渐渐多了起来。太阳快下山了，百鸟归巢。

　　歇脚处的生活像是喀什米尔客栈的缩影。吉姆一头扎进欢快的亚洲似的混乱中。他的需求并不多，因为，喇嘛没有种姓方面的顾忌，所以从最近的售货摊买来的熟食就可以应付。

　　吉姆注意到一辆刚刚驾进歇脚处的家用牛车，车子装修华丽，随行男侍从有八人，其中两个还佩带生锈的马刀。他们中的半数是来自南方的那种双腿纤瘦胡子花白的乌里亚人；另一半是山里人。即使他没有听到两群人之间的争吵，这种组合也已不言而喻了。

The old lady was going south on a visit to a rich relative, probably, a son-in-law, who had sent an escort as a mark of respect.The hill men would be her own people — Kulu or Kangra folk.Something could be got out of meeting the old woman.The Lama would not help.Kim was happy to beg for two.

Kim built his fire as close to the cart as he dared.

"Stand further off! beggar!" was shouted by a hill man.
"Be careful, brother, lest we should curse," said Kim.

The Oriyas laughed, and the Lama raised his head, seeing a hill man spring forward threateningly.

"What is it?" he asked.
The hill man halted as if struck to stone.
"I am saved from a great sin," he stammered.

The hill man drew back to the cart and whispered something. There was dead silence. Then a muttering.

"This goes well," thought Kim.

"When — when — he has eaten," the hill man spoke humbly,"it is requested that the Holly One speak to one who would speak to him."
"When he has eaten, he will sleep," Kim replied loftily.
"Now I will get him his food," said Kim loudly, but ending in a sigh as of faintness.

老太太正往南方去探望一个阔亲戚，可能是个女婿，女婿为示敬意，派来了一组护卫。那些山里人才是她的亲随——库鲁人或者康格拉人。和她见个面也许能有所收获。喇嘛帮不了他的忙，吉姆乐意为师徒俩求布施。

他在尽量靠近牛车的地方升起了篝火。

"站远点，要饭的！"一个山民嚷道。
"当心点，老兄，免得我们诅咒。"吉姆说。

几个乌里亚人哈哈大笑；喇嘛抬起头，那个山里人正气势汹汹地蹿上来。

"怎么回事？"他问道。
山里人停住了，仿佛被吓成个石头人。
"我——我——幸亏得救，没犯下大罪。"他结结巴巴地说。

山里人退回到大车旁，靠着窗帘耳语了几句。先是死一般的寂静，接着一阵窃窃低语。

"这下好了。"吉姆思忖着。

"等——等——等——他吃过饭，"山里人讨好地对吉姆说，"请那位圣者赏脸，有人想和他说话。"

"等他吃过饭，他就要睡觉了，"吉姆爱理不理地说，"现在，我去给他拿吃的来。"这最后一句讲得很响，末尾像是因虚弱而轻叹了一声。

"I — I myself and others of my people will get the food, if permitted."

"It is permitted." said Kim, "Holy One, these people will bring us food."

"The land is good," said the Lama drowsily and slept.

"Let him sleep," said Kim, "but look to it that we are well fed when he wakes. He is a very holy man."

One of the Oriyas said something *contemptuously*.

"He is not a fakir or a beggar," said Kim severely, "he is a Holy Man, above all castes, and I am his chela."

"Come here," said a thin voice behind the curtain.

"Who is that one?"

"A very holy man, coming from far off Tibet!"

"Where in Tibet?"

"From behind the snows. He knows the stars. But he does not do it for money. I am his disciple. When he has eaten, perhaps he will come."

The Lama woke up, and called for Kim."O friend of all the world, he cried in a bewildered voice.

"I come! I come! Holy One," and Kim dashed back where he found the Lama sitting, surrounded by dishes of food.

"Is this thy work?" The Lama inquired.

"There is the virtuous high-born widow of a Hill Rajah,

"我——我自己还有我们的其他人来照料这事好了——要是可以的话。"

"可以,"吉姆说,"圣者,这些人要给我们吃的。"

"这地方可真好。"喇嘛无精打采地咕哝着睡下了。

"先让他睡吧,"吉姆说,"不过等他醒来,保证得让我们好好吃一顿。他是一个大圣人呢。"

有个乌里亚人又轻蔑地说了些什么。

"他不是托钵僧或者乞丐,"吉姆厉声说道,"他是圣人,他高过所有种姓。我是他的弟子。"

"过来!"窗帘后那个细弱单调的声音说道。

"那一位是谁?"

"一个大圣人,是从西藏来的。"

"西藏在哪里呢?"

"从雪山后面。他认识星象,不过他做这些不是为了赚钱,我是他的徒弟。等他吃过饭,他就会过来的。"

"哎,人尽可友!"喇嘛醒了,迷迷糊糊的,喊着找吉姆。

"我来了!圣者,我来了!"他冲到篝火边,看到喇嘛已经被一盘盘饭菜团团围住。

"这也是你做的吗?"喇嘛询问。

"这里有一位出身高贵的、山里王公的遗孀。她要到菩

on a pilgrimage to Bodh Gaya. She sends us those dishes. When you are well-rested she would speak to you."

After the meal, the Lama walked to the cart. Kim would have loved to go, but the Lama did not ask him.

At last the Lama returned. A hill man walked behind him with a wadded cotton quilt, and spread it carefully by the fire.

"She desires greatly that we should go with her to Bodh Gaya — her road being ours.Now since our roads run together for a while, I do not see that we in any way depart from our search, if we accompany her."
"So then we go with her, Holy One?"
"She very greatly desires that I should come."

They slept under the quilts comfortably.

The bright dawn woke men and crows and bullocks together. This was life for Kim, who sat up and yawned, thrilled with delight.

India was awake, and Kim in the middle of it, more awake and more excited than anyone. There was no need to worry about food. All things would be prepared for them and they would be respectfully invited to sit and eat. The old lady was already ordering, scolding and cursing the servants for delays.

提伽耶去朝圣。就是她给我们送来这些饭菜的。等你休息好了，她想和你说说话。"

喇嘛吃完饭朝车子走去。吉姆多想去听一听啊，可是喇嘛没有叫上他。

喇嘛终于回来了。一个山民抱床棉被跟在后面，在篝火旁小心地把棉被铺开。

"她很希望我们和她一块到菩提伽耶，她南下会和我们同路。既然我们会同路几天，我想如果我们和她一起走，也不至于偏离我们的寻找。"

"这么说我们要和她一块儿走了，圣者？"
"她很希望我能同行。"

他们睡进了舒服的棉被。

璀璨的拂晓把男人、母牛和小公牛一块儿唤醒。吉姆坐了起来，打个哈欠，顿时心花怒放。

印度人醒了，而吉姆置身其中，他比任何人都更清醒更兴奋。不用为吃食操心，一切都会为他们准备好的，他们会被恭恭敬敬地邀请坐下来用餐。老太太现在已经开始在吆三喝四、骂骂咧咧了，她也在数落仆人磨磨蹭蹭的。

If Kim had walked proudly, the day before as the disciple of a holy man, today he felt tenfold pride in the semi-royal procession.

The Lama and Kim walked a little to one side. They could hear the old lady talk constantly, bidding the escorts tell her what went on the roads.

如果说吉姆昨天走路时神气十足,因为他是一个圣者的徒弟,那么今天他走起路来更是神气了十倍,因为他行走在一支准皇家行列中。

喇嘛和吉姆稍微偏向一边走着,他们可以听见老太太的喋喋不休。她让亲随告诉她一路上都有些什么事。

5

THE RED BULL

The Lama clicked the beads of his rosary, and began his devotion, grateful for the cool and quiet, and the absence of the dust.

They came out on a broad grazing ground, with a heavy clump of mangoes in the centre. Far across the plain, walking side by side, were four men.

"Soldiers, white soldiers," he said, "Let us see."
"I have never seen white soldiers," said the Lama.
"They do no harm except when they are drunk. Keep behind the tree."

They stepped behind the thick trunks in the cool dark shade of the mango trees. Two men halted, the other two came forward uncertainly.

They were the advance part of a regiment on the march, sent out to mark the camp. They carried five foot sticks with fluttering flags.

60

五
红 牛

喇嘛拨动念珠开始祈祷，面对眼前这一片清凉幽静无烟无尘的乡野，他感到舒爽惬意。

他们面前出现了一片宽阔的牧场，中间是一丛沉甸甸的芒果树。平原远处并排走着四个男子。

"士兵。白人士兵！"他说，"我们来看看吧。"
"我没见过白人士兵。"喇嘛说。
"要是没喝醉酒，他们是不伤人的。躲在这树后吧。"

他们走进清凉阴暗的芒果林，躲在粗大的树干后面。两个小人影停住了；另外两个犹豫不决地继续往前走来。

他们是一支行军中的团先遣队，派来勘察划定扎营地点。他们带着五尺长的标杆，标杆上的旗子随风飘扬。

Calling to each other, they entered the mango-grove, walking heavily.

"It's here — officer's tents under the trees, and the rest of us can stay outside."
"Push the flag in here, then."

Kim stared with his eyes — his breath coming in short and sharp.

"O Holy One!" he gasped. "My horoscope — My prophecy — First come two to make things ready. After them comes the Bull — The Red Bull on the green field? Look! It is he!"

He pointed to the flag that was flapping in the evening breeze not ten feet away. It was an ordinary camp marking-flag, but it had the crest of the regiment — the Red Bull — the crest of the Mavericks — the great Red Bull on a background of Irish green.

"I see," said the lama. "Certainly it is your bull."
"They are white soldiers. The sign of the Bull is the sign of war and armed men."
"True. It is true. Mark," said the Lama.
"I can hear drum — far off!"Soon a sharpness was added.
"Ah! the music," Kim explained. He knew the sound of the regimental band, but it amazed the Lama.

他们拖着沉重的脚步，互相喊着话走进芒果林。

"就在这里，长官的帐篷就搭在这些树下，我们其他人的帐篷可以搭在林外。"

"那就把旗子插在这里吧。"

吉姆睁大眼睛注视着，呼吸急促。

"啊，圣者，"他气喘吁吁地说，"我的天宫图！我的预言！先来两个——仆人——做好准备，跟在他们后面的是公牛——草原上的红公牛？你看！就是它！"

他指着那面正在不足十尺远的地方迎着傍晚的微风徐徐飘动的旗子。那不过是一面普通的标志旗，只是它有这个团的团徽——那只红公牛——小牛团的顶饰——爱尔兰的绿色田野为背景的那只大红公牛。

"看到了，我记起来了，"喇嘛说，"那当然就是你的公牛了。"
"他们是白人士兵。公牛表示战争和武装人员。"

"是这样。真是这样。"喇嘛说。
"我听到有人在远处击鼓！"接着还加进了一阵尖利的声音。
"呵，是音乐。"吉姆解释。他听过军乐队奏乐，可是喇嘛听了却大为惊奇。

At the very end of the plain a heavy, dusty column crawled into sight. The men were route-marching with their baggage and the carts came behind them. The column divided left and right, and soon the plain dotted itself with tents.

"This is magic!" said the Lama.

Another group of men invaded the grove, pitched a huge tent in silence, and took out cooking pots, pans and bundles. Soon the mango-grove turned into an orderly town as they watched.

"Let us go," said the Lama, sinking back afraid, as the fires were lit, and the white officers walked into the mess tent.

"Stand back in the shadow. No one can see beyond the light of the fire," said Kim, his eyes on the flag.

"Look! look! you look! " said the lama, "there comes a 'priest'. "

It was Mr Bennett, the Church of England's Chaplain of the regiment.

"I wish to talk to him about my search."

"Never speak to a white man till he is fed, Let us go back, and after we have eaten, we will come again. It certainly is a Red Bull — my Red Bull."

They ate silently.

平原远处那头，一股浓密的尘烟徐徐前移。士兵带着行李行军。重车辆紧随其后，队伍分成左右两边，接着，草原上星星点点，满是帐篷。

"这简直是妖术！"喇嘛说。

另外一队人拥入林中，不声不响地搭起一个大帐篷。然后拿出做饭用的锅、盆，还有行李。芒果林就在他们眼皮底下变成了一座井然有序的城镇。

"我们走吧。"喇嘛看到一簇簇篝火，白人军官走进当食堂的帐篷，吓得直往后退。

"靠后一点点到暗处。在篝火的火光外面就没人看得见了，"吉姆的眼睛还是注视着那杆旗子。

"瞧！瞧！你瞧！"喇嘛叫了起来，"那边过来一个教士。"

走过来的是班纳特，圣公会的随军牧师。

"我想和他谈谈我的寻找。"
"白人如果没吃饭，千万别跟他讲话，我们还是回歇脚处吧。吃过饭我们再来。那肯定就是红公牛——我的红公牛。"

他们静静地吃饭。

"Now," said Kim, "we will return to that place. You, Holy One, must wait a little way off, as your step is heavier than mine. I am anxious to see more of the Red Bull. This is my search — The search for my Red Bull."

The Lama sat obediently in a little hollow of the ground not a hundred yards from the place.

"Stay till I call," said Kim and flitted away. He lay belly-flat, and wriggled towards the mess tent.

The sole ornament of the centre table was a golden bull — a red gold bull with lowered head, ramping upon a field of Irish green. The Sahibs held out their glasses and drank a toast.

Now the Reverend Arthur Bennet always left the tent after the toast, and being tired after the march his movements were rather abrupt. He stepped on Kim's right shoulder blade, as the boy lay lost in watching the red gold bull on the table.

Kim flinched, rolled sideways, and brought down the priest. But the Reverend was a man of action and caught Kim by the throat, nearly choking him. Kim kicked him desperately in the stomach, and Mr Bennett gasped and doubled, but without relaxing his grip. Silently, he hauled Kim to his tent.

"Why, it's a boy!" he said, "What were you doing there? You are a thief! "

"现在，"吉姆说，"我们再到那个地方去吧，不过，圣者，你必须在稍远的地方等着，因为你的脚步比我沉，我可急着要多看看那头红公牛哩。这是我的寻找——寻找我的红公牛。"

喇嘛顺从地蹲坐在地面的一个浅坑里，这里离芒果林不足一百码。

"待在这儿等我叫你。"吉姆迅速离开了。他匍匐前进，慢慢地靠近灯火通明的食堂帐篷。

餐桌上唯一的摆设是一头金制的公牛——一头红色的纯金公牛，牛头低垂，脚踩着一片爱尔兰的草原。洋大人们朝这个神举起酒杯，乱糟糟地叫喊着。

阿瑟·班纳特牧师总是在祝酒之后就离开食堂，一天的行军把他累得走起路来比往常更加趔趔趄趄。正当吉姆专注地看着桌上他的图腾，牧师突然一脚踩在他的右肩胛上。

吉姆蜷缩起身子，滚到一边，把牧师也拉倒了，但牧师曾经身手敏捷，他一把抓住吉姆的脖子，吉姆拼命朝他肚子踢去。班纳特先生气喘吁吁地团着身子，紧揪住吉姆不松手，悄无声息地把他拖进了自己的帐篷。

"噢，原来是个孩子！"他叫道，"你刚才干什么呢？是个小偷吧。"

As Kim recovered his breath, he made for the doorway, but a long arm caught his neck and closed on the amulet, snapping its string.

"Give it to me! Oh give it to me," Kim cried in English. The Chaplain jumped, "Why, do you speak English? Little boys who steal are beaten. You know that?"

"I do not — I did not steal. Oh, give it to me. It is my charm."

The chaplain went to the door, and called aloud. A fattish, clean-shaven man appeared.

"I want your advice, Father Victor," said Bennett. "I found this boy in the dark outside the mess tent. I believe him to be a thief, but he talks in English, and attaches some sort of value to a charm round his neck."

"We'll look first," said father Victor, and leisurely rolled out poor Kimball O'Hara's birth certificate. On the back O'hara had scrawled. "Look after the boy. Please look after the boy," signing his name and regimental number in full.

"Do you know what these things are?" asked father Victor.

"They are mine, I'll go away," said Kim.

"Kimball O'Hara! And his son!"

Father Victor stepped forward quickly and opened the front of Kim's garment. "You see, Mr Bennett, He is not black. What's your name?"

吉姆缓过气来朝门口冲去，但一只长臂迅速伸出来揪住他的脖子，拉断了护身符的带子。

"还给我。哦，还给我。"吉姆喊。这些都是用英文讲的，牧师跳了起来："怎么，你会讲英语吗？偷东西的小孩是要挨揍的。这你应该知道。"

"我没有，我刚才没偷。哦，还给我吧，那是我的护身符。"

他走到帐篷门口喊起来。一个脸刮得光光的胖子出现了。

"我有事向您请教，维克多神甫，"班纳特说，"我在食堂帐篷外的暗处发现了这个男孩，我想他是个小偷。不过他会讲英语，又很珍视他脖子上挂的护身符。"

"我们得先看看，"维克多神甫边说边从容不迫地把可怜的吉姆波尔·欧哈拉那张出生证明摊开，在这反面，欧哈拉写着："照顾这个孩子，请照顾这个孩子。"还完完整整地签上他的名字，并附上他那个团的番号。

维克多神甫说："你知道这些是什么东西吗？"

"它是我的，我想走了。"

"吉姆波尔·欧哈拉！他的儿子！"

维克多神甫快步上前，揭开吉姆的上衣前襟："你瞧，班纳特，他的皮肤是白色的，你叫什么名字？"

"Kim."

"Or Kimball?"

"Perhaps. Will you let me go away?"

"What else?"

Slowly, piece by piece, Kim's story came out.

"Go on, Kim," murmured Father Victor.

"I did not steal. Besides, I am just now disciple to a very holy man. He is sitting outside. Will you hurt him, if I call him now? He can witness all things, and knows I am not a thief."

"We had better invite the holy man. He may know something," said Bennet.

Mr Bennett marched Kim off, with a firm hand on his shoulder.

"吉姆。"

"或许是吉姆波尔吧？"

"也许吧，要不要让我走呢？"

"还叫什么？"

慢慢地，吉姆的故事一点点明朗了。

"说吧，吉姆。"维克多神甫低声说。

"我刚才真没偷。再说，我现在还是一个大僧人的弟子呢。他就坐在外头。要是我这就喊他一声，你们会伤害他吗？他可以证明我说的都是真话，他知道我不是小偷。"

"我们最好把他的同伙请来。他也许会知道点什么。"班纳特说。

他一手紧抓着吉姆的肩膀走了。

6

NEW LIFE FOR KIM

"The search is at an end for me, I have found the Bull, but God knows what comes next. Come with the thin man to the fat priest's tent. They cannot talk Hindi," said Kim.

Dignified and unsuspicious, the Lama strode into the little tent.

"What was the end of the search? What gift has the Red Bull brought?" The Lama addressed Kim in Urdu. "He says — what are you going to do?" Kim told Bennett.

"I do not see what concern has the 'fakir' with the boy," Bennett began.

"But we might as well tell him what we are going to do. He doesn't look like a villain," said father Victor."Now Kimball, I wish you to tell this man what I say — word for word."

"Holy One, the thin man, who looks like a camel, says that I am the son of a Sahib. O, it's time. I knew it since my birth, but he could only tell after reading the amulet's paper. He thinks a Sahib is always a Sahib. They intend to keep me

六

吉姆的新生活

"我的寻找结束了，我找到了公牛，可是神才知道接下去怎么样。跟这个瘦子去那个胖教士的帐篷里吧。"吉姆说。

喇嘛举止端庄毫无顾忌地大踏步走进小帐篷里。

"寻找的结果怎么样？那只红公牛带来了什么礼物？"喇嘛用乌尔都语问吉姆。"他说，'你们打算怎么办？'"吉姆对班纳特说。

"我看不出这个托钵僧和这孩子有什么关系。"班纳特说话了。

"不过我们不妨告诉这位老人我们打算怎么做。他看起来就不像个坏人。行了，吉姆波尔，我要你来告诉这个人我说的话—— 一字不差地告诉他。"维克多神甫说。

"圣者，那个看上去像头骆驼的瘦傻子说，我是洋大人的儿子，这是真的。我打生下来就知道这事了，不过他只能看过我脖子上的护身符才搞清楚。他说洋大人永远是洋大人，他们想把我留在团里或者送我进学校。我可以在这里待

in this regiment or send me to school. I may spend one night there, then I will run away and return to you."

"But tell them you are my disciple. Tell them how we met. Tell them of our search, and surely, they will let you go."

"What is it," said father Victor, as he watched the Lama's face. The priest felt overcome with feeling.

Kim translated in his own mind from vernacular to English, and related the story of Lord Buddha's arrow, the river and the search.

"You can't go in that old man's company. It would have been different, Kim, if you were not a soldier's son. Tell him the regiment will take care of you, and make you as good a man as your — as good a man as can be."

"They say," said Kim to the Lama, "that my prophecy is now complete, and I am just making a *pretence* of agreement. Then I will slip away and come to you. So Holy One, keep with the Kulu woman, till I come back. My father must have been some great person. So if they raise me, good. If not, then, good again. I will run back to you.Oh. Yes,"said the boy, "I have told him everything."

"Then why should he wait?" said the chaplain.

"Give him time. May be he's fond of the lad," said Father Victor.

The Lama covered his face, and nervously rattled his rosary. Kim sat near him, and held a fold of his clothing.

74

上一夜或者再一夜。然后我就逃走去找你。"

"可是你得告诉他们你是我的弟子,告诉他们我们是怎么碰到的,告诉他们我们这是去寻找,这样他们就会让你走的。"

"那是什么事儿呢?"维克多神甫看着喇嘛的脸,不无同情地问道。

吉姆在脑子里将土话翻译成英语,把他和世尊菩萨的箭河和这次寻找联系起来。

"你不能跟着那个老人。吉姆,如果你不是个士兵的孩子,那就不一样了。告诉他,团里会照看你,会让你成为一个男子汉,像你的——像你能达到的水平。"

"他们说,"吉姆对喇嘛说,"我的预言已经应验了,现在我假装同意,然后我会溜走,回到你的身边,所以圣者,你就跟着那个库鲁女人,一直到我回去。我父亲以前一定是个大官。所以如果他们培养我,那很好。如果不,那也好,我就跑去找你。哦,是的,"孩子说,"我已经把一切都告诉他了。"

"那他为什么还在等?"班纳特说。
"给他时间吧,或许他喜欢这孩子。"维克多神甫说。

喇嘛把脸盖住,惶恐不安地拨动念珠。吉姆在他身旁坐下,拉住他僧袍上的一道皱层。

"The boy is a Sahib. So he must go back to his own people."

"I do not understand the customs of the white men. This boy will be taken from me. They will make a Sahib of him. Woe to me! How shall I find my river?"

Kim explained the Lama's distress, and added.

"I wish I had not come here to find the Red Bull. I do not want it."

"Good heavens, I do not know how to *console* him," said Father Victor. "He can't take the boy away with him, and yet he's a good man."

They listened to each other's breathing. Then the Lama raised his head, and looked across them into space and emptiness.

"I am the follower of the way," he said bitterly. "The sin is mine, and the punishment is mine. I made myself believe that you had been sent to aid me in my search — so my heart went out to you. But this is all Illusion. I had stepped away from the way, my chela. It is not your fault. Now I am full of sorrow because you are being taken away from me, and my river is far from me. I had broken the law. I can see that the sign of the Red Bull was for both of us. All desire is red — and evil. I will do *penance* and find my river alone."

"At least go back to the Kulu woman," said Kim, "or you will be lost on the roads. She will feed you till I come back."

"这孩子是个洋大人,因此他必须回到他自己人那边去。"

"我不懂白人的规矩。这孩子要从我身边给夺走了。他们要把我的徒弟培养成洋大人,我真不幸啊。我怎么能找到我的河呢？"

吉姆理解喇嘛的忧伤,他接着说:

"要是我没有来这里找那只红公牛和那些事就好了,我不要公牛了。"

"天哪,我真不知道该怎样安慰他,"维克多神甫说,"他不能把孩子带走,不过他倒是一个好人。"

他们静听着彼此的呼吸,而后喇嘛抬起头来,目光越过他们,望入空白和虚无中。

"我还是个讲道的呢,"他悲伤地说,"是我造了孽,我该遭报应。我让自己相信你是奉命来帮助我寻找的。于是我疼爱你,可这全是幻象。我偏离了正道,我的弟子。这不是你的错。现在我很难过,因为你要被夺走了,而我那条河还远着呢。我冒犯了佛法。我明白了,红公牛的星象点是你的也是我的。所有的贪欲都是赤色的,都是邪恶的。我要苦修来赎罪,亲自去找我的河。"

"至少回库鲁女人那里去,"吉姆说,"要不你会迷路的。她会给你吃的,直到我回到你身边。"

The Lama waved a hand to show that the matter was settled in his mind.

"Now," his tone altered as he turned to Kim, "what will they do with you?"

"Make me a Sahib — so they think."

"Of what sort? tell me before I go, for it is not a small thing to make a child."

"You will be sent to school," said Father Victor. "Later on, we shall see Kimball, I suppose you'd like to be a soldier?"

Kim shook his head violently. "I will not be a soldier."

"You will be what you are told to be, and be grateful for our help," said Bennett sternly.

"Ask them how much money do they need for a wise and suitable teaching? And in what city is that teaching given?"

Kim translated and Father Victor answered. "The regiment would pay for you at the army orphanage. But the best school is. St. Xavier's in Lucknow."

"He wants to know how much?" said Kim calmly.

"Rs 200 to 300 a year."

"He says , Write that name and the money upon a paper and give it to him. And he says you must write your name below it, because he is going to write a letter in some days to you. He says you are a good man, and he is going away now." The Lama rose suddenly. "I follow my search," he cried, and was gone.

　　喇嘛摆了摆手表示对这件事他已打定了主意。

　　"现在，"他转身面对吉姆，语气也变了，"他们会把你怎么样？"

　　"把我培养成一个洋大人，他们是这样想的。"

　　"什么样的洋人？在我走之前你得告诉我，因为培养孩子可不是件小事。"

　　"你会被送进学校，"维克多神甫说，"吉姆波尔，我猜想你应该喜欢当兵吧？"

　　吉姆拼命地摇头："我不愿当兵。"

　　"叫你当什么你就要当什么，"班纳特严肃地说，"你应该感激我们对你的帮助才对。"

　　"问问他们，接受一种有智慧又适当的教育得花多少钱？还有，在哪个城市有这样的教育？"

　　吉姆翻译，维克多神甫回答："在军人孤儿院，整个费用全由团里付。不过，最好的教育当然是勒克瑙的圣查维尔学校。"

　　"他想知道要多少钱？"吉姆平静地说。

　　"一年两三百个卢比。"

　　"他说，把那个学校的名字和多少钱写在一张纸上，然后给他。他还说你必须把你的名字写在下边，因为他有时会给你来信，他说你是个好人。他要走了。"喇嘛突然站起身来。"我要继续去寻找。"他大声说着走了。

The Lama disappeared silently. No sentry stopped him.

Kim settled himself on the Chaplain's cot, comforted by the thought that the Lama would stay with the Rajput woman from Kulu.

Father Victor and Mr Bennett planned his future, while he felt sleepy. All this was new and fascinating. Meantime, if the Sahibs were to be impressed, he would do his best to impress them.

The regiment would go on to Umballa, and he would be sent to a place called Sanawar.

"His Buddhist friend had taken my name and address," said Father Victor. "I can't quite make out whether he will pay for the boy's education, or he's planning some magic."

"But you will not go to Sanawar," said Kim.

"But we will go to Sanawar. That's the order of the Commander in Chief, who's more important than O'Hara's son."

"You will not go to Sanawar. You will go to the war."

There was a shout of laughter from the full tent.

"We hope to go to the war sometime."

They did not know what he knew of the talk in the Verandah at Umballa.

外边没有查问，喇嘛已无影无踪了。

吉姆坐到牧师的床上。想到喇嘛会跟那个库鲁来的拉奇谱特妇人在一起，他就安心了。

维克多神甫和班纳特规划着吉姆的未来，这一切都很新奇有趣，不过吉姆困了。这期间如果洋大人们需要得到什么印象，他会尽力让他们留下印象的。

这个团要继续开往乌姆巴拉，吉姆将被送往一个叫萨纳瓦的地方。

维克多神甫说："他那位佛教朋友拿了我的名字和地址，我不大明白他是要为这孩子支付学费呢，还是在准备什么巫术。"

"可是你们不是去萨纳瓦。"吉姆说。

"可是我们就是去萨纳瓦，那是总司令的命令，他比欧哈拉的儿子重要一点。"

"你们不是去萨纳瓦，你们是去打仗。"

帐篷里一阵哄堂大笑。

"我们倒是希望什么时候能打打仗。"

他们不知道他在乌姆巴拉的走廊里听来的那番谈话。

"I know you are not at war now. But as soon as you get to Umballa you will be sent to war — a new war. It is a war of eight thousand men and guns."

"Do you add prophecy to your other gifts? Take him along sergeant."

An hour later, Kim sat newly washed all over, in a horrible stiff suit.

Very early next morning, the tents came down, as the Mavericks marched to Umballa. He knew he was being closely watched, Father Victor on one side, and Mr Bennett on the other.

In the forenoon a camel rider handed the colonel a letter. Half a mile in the rear, he could hear joyful shoutings. Then someone slapped his back. "Tell us how did you know. Father, see if you can make him tell you."

"Now, my son, your prophecy of last night has come true. We are to take a train at Umballa, and go to the Front. We are going to war."

"Of course you are. I told you last night."

"You did. But how did you know?"

Kim's eyes sparkled. He shut his lips, nodded his head, and kept silent, as if he knew more.

"It must have been a bazaar rumour," said the Chaplain. "The thing was decided within the last forty-eight hours."

"我知道你们现在不是在打仗；不过你们一到乌姆巴拉，马上就会被派去打仗，是新的战争——有八千人参加的战争，还有大炮。"

"你是否把预言作为你的另外的天赋？带他去换上军士的装束。"

一个小时后，吉姆坐着，他浑身上下刚洗过，穿着一套扎手扎脚的军服。

第二天一大早，那些营帐就被拆除了，小牛团起程开往乌姆巴拉。吉姆知道他被严密监视着——维克多神甫在一边，班纳特先生在另一边。

午前时分，一个骆驼骑兵过来，把一封信交给上校。吉姆听到在相隔半英里远处传来一阵欣喜的喧闹声。接着有人拍了拍他的背："告诉我们你怎么会知道的？亲爱的神甫，看看你能不能让他说出实话来。"

"听着，我的孩子，你昨晚的预言应验了。我们明天在乌姆巴拉搭乘火车，开赴前线。我们要去打仗了。"

"你们当然是去打仗。我昨天晚上就说了。"

"你是说了，可是你是怎么知道的呢？"

吉姆两眼闪亮。他闭上双唇，点了点头，沉默不语，一副讳莫如深的样子。

"多半是市井流言嘛，"上校说，"这事可是四十八小时内才决定的。"

7

KIM'S SCHOOL — AND LETTER

For the rest of the day Kim found himself important enough to be discussed by the few hundred men in the camp. The story of his appearance in the camp, his parentage, and his prophecy, had made news. There seemed no sign of hardwork.

But by next morning they were on the platform in perfect shape and condition and Kim was left behind with the sick, women, and boys, shouting farewells excitedly as the train drew away.

Life as a Sahib had been amusing so far. Then they marched him back in charge of a drummer-boy to empty barracks. He curled himself on a stripped cot and went to sleep.

An angry man walked heavily across and woke him up. He was the schoolmaster. That was enough for Kim to retire into his shell.

七

吉姆的学校——还有
一封信

在这一天里,吉姆发现自己成了军营里数百名士兵谈论的人物。关于他怎么来到军营里,他的身世,还有他的预言,全都被一五一十地传开了。

第二天一早,他们一个个戎装整齐精神抖擞地集合在站台上,吉姆和那些病人、妇女以及男孩一起被留了下来。当一列列火车徐徐开动时,他跟大家一样,高声道别。

洋大人的生活到现在为止快乐有趣。然后他们让小鼓手负责把他送回空荡荡的营房。他在帆布床上蜷缩成一团睡着了。

有个人气咻咻地拖着沉重的步子走来,把吉姆叫醒,他是教员。对吉姆来说,这就够了。

"I do not know anything. Go away!" said Kim. Hereupon, the man caught him by the ear, and dragged him to a room in a far-off wing. Twelve drummer boys were sitting on benches. He was told to sit still. This he managed very well. The man explained something on the blackboard and drew white lines with chalk.

Kim continued his interrupted nap. Kim had been trying to avoid this school and disciplined life up to now. Suddenly, a beautiful idea occurred to him.

As soon as the man dismissed the class, Kim was the first to spring into the open sunshine. "Here you! Halt! Stop!" said a high voice at his heels.

"I've got to look after you. My orders are not to let you out of my sight. Where are you going?"

Kim hated this fat and freckled, fourteen-year old drummer boy, who had hung round him all afternoon.

"How near can we go?"
"We can go as far as that tree down the road."
"Then I will go there."
"Alright. I'm not going. It's too hot. I can watch you from here."

Kim hailed a sweeper. The boy replied insolently in Urdu, thinking that the European boy would not follow it. But Kim's quick reply made him aware of his error.

“我什么也不知道，滚开！”吉姆说。那人一听，揪住他的耳朵，把他拖到远处边房的一个屋里。十二个小鼓手坐在长板凳上，吉姆被告知要老老实实坐着。这一点他表现得非常出色。那人用粉笔在黑板上解释了些什么。

吉姆继续他那场被打断的睡梦。他一直在极力躲避学校生活和清规戒律。突然，他有了一个美妙的想法。

那人一宣布下课，吉姆就第一个跳跃着冲进阳光里。“嘿！你！站住！停下！”一个声音紧跟在他身后高喊着。

“我得看着你。我奉命盯紧你。你去哪里？”

那个一整个下午都不离前后的小鼓手是个十四岁、满脸雀斑的小胖子，吉姆真是对他烦透了。

“我们可以走多远呢？”
“最远到那棵树。”
“那我就走到那里。”
“好吧，我可不去。天太热了。我可以从这里看着你。”

吉姆向一个清洁工打招呼，那人立即傲慢地回敬了一句乌尔都语，满以为这个欧洲男孩听不懂，可吉姆的迅速答复使他意识到自己错了。

"Go to the nearest letter-writer and tell him to come here. I would write a letter."

The sweeper hurried off in haste. "There is a white boy in the barracks who is not a white boy."Stammered the sweeper to the first letter-writer. "He is waiting for you under a tree. He needs you."

Kim danced with impatience as the letter-writer came into sight, and cursed him for being slow.

"What kind of white boy are you?"

"That shall be said in the letter to Mahbub Ali, the horse dealer in Kashmir Serai at Lahore. He is my friend."

"Wonder on Wonder!" murmured the letter-writer. "To be written in Hindi?"

"Certainly. To Mahbub Ali."

"Begin.I came down with the old man to Umballa, and carried the news of the horse's pedigree. We then went on foot to Benaras, but on the third day we found a certain regiment. I went into the camp and was caught. Through my charm they found I was the son of a man in the regiment : according to the prophecy of the Red Bull, which you know. Now, they are sending me to school, and beat me. My clothes are heavy, and my heart is heavy too, although I am a Sahib. I do not like the air and water here. Come and help me, Mahbub Ali, or send me money, for I don't have enough to pay the writer of this letter."

"到最近的写信人那里去，叫他来这里，我想写封信。"

清洁工匆匆走了。"军营那边有个白人男孩，他不是白人的孩子。"他结结巴巴地对写信人说，"他在树下等你，他需要你的帮助。"

当写信人出现时，吉姆正急得直跺脚。对他的姗姗来迟，吉姆破口大骂。

"你是个什么种类的白人孩子呢？"
"这事会在写给马哈布·阿里的信里会说起，他是拉合尔的喀什米尔客栈的马贩子。他是我的朋友。"
"怪上加怪！"写信人喃喃低语，"用印地语写吗？"

"当然。给马哈布·阿里。"

开始，我和那老人家南下到了乌姆巴拉，把马的血统那条消息送出去。我们走路到贝纳勒斯，不过第三天我们碰上了一个团。我进他们的营帐里被抓住了，看过我的护身符，他们发现我是这个团里一个人的儿子，跟红公牛的预言相符，这你知道。他们正把我送进学校，还打我，我的衣服很沉，心也很沉，尽管我是洋大人，可我不喜欢这里的空气和水。马哈布·阿里，来帮帮我吧，或者寄点钱来，因为我的钱不够付给写这封信的人。

The writer grunted, but took out a stamp and sealed the letter. Mahabub Ali's was a powerful name in Umballa.

"Pay me twice over, when the money comes,"shouted the letter writer over his shoulder.

Three days of torment passed in the big, echoing white rooms. When he wished to sleep, he was instructed how to fold up his clothes and set out his boots. Bugles woke him at dawn, and the schoolmaster gave him meaningless lessons after breakfast, beating him without cause. The drummer-boy was his guard. This strong loneliness preyed on him. He wondered whether Mahbub Ali would visit him next time he came south with the horses.

On the fourth morning, they had gone out together, he, attended by the drummer, towards the Umballa racecourse. The drummer-boy returned alone, weeping, with news that young O'Hara had called out to a dark man on a horseback. The man had a red beard, and he had picked up O'Hara, and borne him off at full gallop.

This news came to Father Victor. He was already astonished by a letter from the Jain Temple at Benaras, with a banker's note for Rs 300.

Three miles off, on Umballa racecourse, Mahbub Ali on a grey Kabuli horse, with Kim in front of him, was saying.

写信人嘟囔着，但还是拿出一张邮票来，把信封上。毕竟，马哈布·哈里在乌姆巴拉是个有名气的人。

"等钱寄来，你得付我两倍。"那人转过头大声说。

沉闷乏味的三天在几间宽敞、响着回声的白色房间里度过。当他想睡觉时，他们教他怎么叠衣服摆靴子。军号声把他叫醒，吃过早餐，那个教员给他上毫无意义的课，然后平白无故地打他。那个小鼓手紧随左右。他心头笼罩着极度的孤单，他怀疑马哈布·阿里第二天是否会赶着马群到南方来看他。

第四天上午，他们一起去乌姆巴拉赛马场，返回时却只有小鼓手一人，他哭哭啼啼地报告说，小欧哈拉跟一个骑马而来的红胡子黑鬼打了个招呼，那人抓起小欧哈拉疾驰而去。维克多神甫听到了这一消息。

一封寄自贝纳勒斯特丹卡寺的信已经让他深为震惊，信内附有一张金额为三百卢比的支票。

在三英里外的乌姆巴拉赛马场上，马哈布·阿里骑着一匹灰色的高布尔种马，吉姆坐在他前面，马哈布说道：

"But, little friend of all the world, there is my name and my honour to be considered. All officers and all regiments know Mahbub Ali. How can I take you away? If I let you run away, how will I explain that? They would put me in jail. Be patient. Once a Sahib, always a Sahib, when you are a man — who knows? Will you be grateful to Mahbub Ali?"

"Take me beyond the guards. Let me change my clothes. Give me money and I will go to Benares and be with my Lama again. I do not want to be a Sahib."

"Hi! Mahbub, you old rascal, pull up!" cried a voice, and an Englishman raced alongside on a little polo-pony. I've been chasing you over half the country. Is that Kabuli horse of yours for sale?"

"I have some young ponies come up, made by heaven for the difficult and delicate game of polo. He has no equal."

"What have you got there?"

"A boy," said Mahbub seriously. "He was being beaten by another boy. His father was a white soldier in Lahore, and this boy played with my horses as a youngster. Now, I think they want to make him a soldier. He has been just caught by his father's regiment last week. I don't think he wants to be a soldier. I am taking him for a ride. Tell me where your barracks are, and I'll reach you there."

"Let me go, and I can find the barracks alone."

"But if you run away, who will say it is not my fault."

"不过，人尽可友小朋友，还得顾及我的脸面和声誉嘛。团里的所有军官都认识马哈布·阿里。我怎么能把你带走，要是让你逃走，我又该怎么解释，他们会把我抓进监狱的。忍忍吧，一旦你是洋大人，就会一直是洋大人。等你成为男子汉的时候——谁知道呢——你就会感激马哈布·阿里的。"

"带我离开士兵，让我换一下衣服，给我一点钱，我要去贝纳勒斯找我的喇嘛。我不想当洋大人。"

"嘿！马哈布，你这个老家伙，停下！"一个声音叫道，一个英国人骑匹打马球用的小马追了上来。"我跑了大半个跑马场追你。要卖的是那匹高布尔马吗？"

"我还有一些小矮种马，是老天专门为精致而难打的马球赛准备的，天下无双。"
"你那边是个什么东西呢？"

"是个孩子，"马哈布一本正经地说，"他被另外一个孩子揍了一顿，他父亲是拉合尔的白人士兵，这孩子从小就来找我的马玩。我想他们现在是要让他当兵。他上星期刚刚被他们逮住。依我看，他并不想当兵。我带他出来骑马兜兜风。告诉我你的营房在哪里，我会把你送到那里。"

"放我走吧，我自己能回营房。"
"可是万一你跑了，人家不会怪我吗？"

"He will run back to his dinner," said the Englishman.

"He was born in the land. He has friends. He only needs to change his clothes and he will be a low-caste Hindu boy."

The Englishman looked at the boy closely.

Mahbub went on, "They will send him to school and put heavy boots on his feet, and wrap him in these clothes. Then he will forget all he knows. Now which is your barrack?"

Kim pointed, unable to speak.

"Perhaps he will make a good soldier," said Mahbub. "He will make a good orderly at least. I sent him to deliver a message once from Lahore — concerning the pedigree of a white stallion."

Mahbub stared deliberately at the Englishman, who stared as deliberately at Kim, who shook with anger and said nothing.

"Ah," said the Englishman, "who is making the boy a soldier. The regiment that found him, and specially the priest of the regiment."

"There is the priest!" Kim choked as Father Victor came down the verandah to meet them.

"O'hara!" he cried as Kim slid down and slid helplessly before him.

"他会跑回去吃饭的。"英国人说。

"他生在这里，他有的是朋友。只消给他换身衣服，他就变成了一个低种姓的印度孩子了。"

英国人仔细地看着这孩子。

马哈布接着往下说："他们会送他上学，给他双脚套上笨重的靴子，再拿这些服装把他团团围住。这样一来，他就会把他知道的一切忘个一干二净。得了，前面的营房哪个是你住的？"

吉姆朝前指，他说不出来。

"也许他会成为一个出色的士兵，"马哈布说，"至少能成为一个出色的传令兵。我曾让他送过一封从拉合尔来的信，是关于一匹白种马的血统证明。"

马哈布紧紧盯着英国人，英国人审视着吉姆，吉姆生气地摇摇头，什么都没说。

"噢，"英国人说，"是谁要把这孩子培养成士兵呢？找到他的那个团，特别是团里的洋人牧师？"

"牧师就在那里！"吉姆手指神甫，他正从走廊朝他们走来。

"欧哈拉！"他大声说道。这时吉姆滑下马来，无助地站到他面前。

95

8

COLONEL CREIGHTON'S ROLE

"Good Morning, Father," the Englishman said cheerfully. "I'm Colonel Creighton. I should have called before this. That boy interests me. Can you tell me anything about him?"

"Can I tell you?" puffed Father Victor. "I'm bursting to tell someone! Excuse me a minute. I'll get the *documents* of the case."

Colonel Creighton dropped into a chair, from where he could see Kim and Mahbub Ali clearly.

"If through me the favour of this bold and wise Colonel Sahib comes to you, and you are raised to honour, what thanks will you give Mahbub Ali when you are a man?"

"I begged you to let me take the road — again, and here you have sold me back to the English."

八

上校克莱顿的身份

"早安，神甫，"英国人愉快地问候道，"早就想过来拜访了。我是克莱顿。我对这个男孩很感兴趣，你能告诉我关于他的一些事吗？"

"我能跟您讲吗？"维克多神甫无可奈何地说，"我很想找个人聊聊呢，请稍等几分钟，我会找到有关这件事的一些资料。"

克莱顿上校坐进一张椅子里，从那儿可以清楚地看见吉姆和马哈布·阿里。

"要是因为我而使这位有名望有智慧的上校大人看重你，当你成了堂堂男子汉，你要怎么感谢马哈布·阿里呢？"

"我求你让我重新上路吧，是你把我回卖给英国人。"

Father Victor waved some letters before the Colonel. After fifteen minutes, Father Victor could be seen answering questions energetically or talking to the Colonel.

"Now I have told you everything that I know about the boy from the beginning to the end. Have you ever heard such a story?"

"At any rate, the old man has sent the money," said the Colonel. "If the Lama, fails to pay next year, what then?"

"If he says he will pay — he'll pay, dead or alive. My advice is to send the boy to Lucknow. Put the blame on me. I strongly recommend sending the boy to St. Xavier's. I've got to go to Lucknow next week. I'll look after the boy on the way. He can pass as a soldier's orphan, so the railway fare will be saved. Give him in charge of my servants."

"You're a good man."

"Not in the least. The Lama has sent us money for a definite end. We can't return it. We shall have to do what he says. That's settled, then. Shall I say, next Tuesday? That's only three days.

"I can't thank you enough. I must get back. Good heavens! Old Mahbub Ali here still?" He raised his voice. "Well, what is it?"

"Regarding the young horse," said Mahbub. When a *colt* is born to be a polo-pony, and follows the ball without teaching — it knows the game by *intuition*, then it is a great wrong to use the colt to draw a heavy cart."

"So say I also, Mahbub. The colt will be entered for polo

维克多神甫在上校面前晃动着一些信件，十五分钟后，可以看见他正在兴奋地回答上校的问题或是和上校聊天。

"现在我已经把我所知道的关于这孩子的一切原原本本全告诉您了。您听说过类似的事吗？"

"不管怎么说，那老人家把钱寄来了。"上校说，"万一喇嘛明年付不了钱，会怎样呢？"

"如果他说付钱，他就会付的——不管是死是活。我建议下周把孩子送到勒克瑙。怪就怪我吧，我极力主张把孩子送到圣查维尔学校。我下周要去勒克瑙。我会一路关照这孩子，他可以带上军人孤儿的通行证，这样就省去车费了。把他交给我那些仆人们就是了。"

"你真是个好人。"

"那倒不是，是喇嘛寄钱来，而且用途明确。我们又不好把钱寄回去。我们只得照他说的去做了。就这么定了。下星期二怎么样？只剩三天了。"

"我对您感激不尽。我必须回去了。老天，老马哈布还在这里。"他提高了声音。"喂，有什么事儿吗？"

"关于那匹小马，"马哈布说，"如果一匹小马天生是打马球用的，不用教，它就能紧跟着球跑；如果他凭灵性就知道游戏技巧，那么训练这匹马去拉大车就是大错特错！"

"我也是这么说的，马哈布。这匹小马只能用来打马球。

only. (These fellows think of nothing but horses, Father.) I'll see you tomorrow Mahbub."

The horse-dealer saluted.

"Be patient, Friend of all the World," he whispered to the suffering Kim. "Your fortune is made. You are going to Lucknow."

"Listen to me," said the Colonel from the verandah, speaking in the vernacular. "In three days you will go with me to Lucknow, seeing and hearing new things. So stay here for three days, and do not run away. You will go to school at Lucknow."

"Shall I meet my Holy One there?" asked Kim.

"At least Lucknow is nearer to Benares than Umballa. May be you can go under my protection. Mahbub Ali knows this. If you return to the road, he will be angry. Remember, much has been told to me, and I do not forget."

"I will wait," said Kim, as the bugles blew for dinner.

In the afternoon the red faced schoolmaster told Kim that he had been "struck off the strength," which conveyed no meaning to him till he was ordered to go and play. He ran to the bazaar, and found the young letter — writer to whom he owed a stamp.

"Now I pay," said Kim proudly, "and I need another letter to be written."

（神甫，这些家伙除了马以外这世界上的事他们什么也不想）我们明天见，马哈布。"

马贩子敬了个礼。

"忍耐些，人尽可友，"他对愁眉苦脸的吉姆低声细语。"你交上好运了，你就要到勒克瑙去。"

"听我说，"上校从走廊上用图画对吉姆说，"再过三天你就和我一起到勒克瑙，一路上能耳闻目睹新鲜事。所以呀，安静地在这待上三天，别跑走。你将到勒克瑙去上学。"

"我能见到那位圣者吗？"吉姆问。
"勒克瑙至少比乌姆巴拉离贝纳勒斯更近些。也许你可以在我的保护下去见他。这事马哈布·阿里知道，要是你再溜回大路上去他会不高兴的。记住——他们告诉我许多事，我不会忘记的。"
"那么，我会在这里等着。"吉姆说。这时响起了用膳号。

下午那个红脸教员告诉吉姆他已经"从名册上除名"，直到有人下令让他离开去玩耍，吉姆才明白这是什么意思。他跑到街市上，找到那个他还欠着一张邮票的年轻的写信人。

"现在我付钱，"吉姆骄傲地说，"我还要再写封信。"

"Mahbub Ali is in Umballa," said the writer.

"This is not to Mahbub, but to a priest. Take your pen and write quickly. To Teshoo Lama, the Holy One from Tibet, seeking for a river, who is now in the Temple of the Tirthankaras at Benares. Take more! In three days I am going to Lucknow. The name of the school is St. Xaviers. I do not know where the school is, but it is at Lucknow."

The pen scratched busily. Then the man raised his head. "Who is watching us across the street?"

Kim looked up and saw Colonel Creighton in his tennis outfit.

"He is calling me," said Kim.
"What are you doing?" asked the Colonel when Kim reached him.
"I am not running away. I am sending a letter to my Holy One at Benares."
The Colonel smiled, "I have left my cigarette case in the priest's verandah. Bring it to my house this evening."
"Where is your house?" asked Kim. His quick wit told him he was being tested.
"Ask anyone in the bazaar," said the Colonel and left.

Kim turned to the letter-writer — "That is all, except thrice over, Come to me! Come to me! Come to me!"

"马哈布·阿里就在乌姆巴拉呀。"写信人说。

"不是写给马哈布，而是写给一个和尚的。把笔拿过来赶快写。给德寿喇嘛，这位圣者来自西藏，正在寻找一条河，现住在贝纳勒斯的特丹卡寺里。三天后我将到勒克瑙。学校的名字是圣查维尔。我不知道学校在哪里，反正是在勒克瑙。"

笔沙沙地写个不停。然后那人抬起头来："在街对面看着我们的那个人是谁？"

吉姆抬头一看，看到身着网球裤的克莱顿上校。

"他叫我过去呢。"吉姆说。
"你在干什么？"吉姆跑上前时，上校问道。

"我不是想逃走。我寄封信到贝纳勒斯给我的那个圣者。"

上校笑了："我把雪茄烟盒落在神甫的走廊里了。傍晚你把它送到我房屋去。"
"你住在哪里呢？"吉姆问。他心思敏捷，一下就明白这是在考验他。
"到大街上随便问问吧。"上校说着就走掉了。

吉姆返回写信人这边："信上要写的就这些。写上三遍：来找我！来找我！来找我！"

He rose to go, and as an afterthought asked who was the angry-faced Sahib.

"Oh, he is only Creighton Sahib — a very foolish Sahib without a regiment."

"What is his work?"

"God knows. He is always buying horses which he cannot ride. The horse-dealers call him the father of fools, because he is so easily cheated. Mahbub Ali says he is madder than most Sahibs."

"Oh," said Kim, and left. Fools, he thought that fools are not given information which leads to calling out eight thousand men besides guns. The Commander in Chief of the Army does not talk to fools, as Kim had heard him talk. Mahbub Ali's tone changed every time he mentioned the Colonel's name and this set Kim thinking that there was a mystery somewhere.

Mahbub Ali probably spied for the Colonel, as Kim had spied for Mahbub Ali. Like the horse-dealer, the Colonel evidently respected people who did not show themselves to be too clever.

He was happy that he had not betrayed his knowledge of the Colonel's house. On his return to the barracks, when he found that no cigarette case had been left behind, he beamed with delight. Here was a man after his own heart — an indi-

他站起来准备走了，然后像想起什么似的问："那个满脸不高兴的洋大人到底是谁呀？"

"噢，他不就是克莱顿大人吗——一个愚不可及的、不属于任何团的洋大人。"

"那他做什么事呢？"

"天晓得。他老是买一些骑不了的马，马贩子都说他是个傻瓜之父，因为他很容易上当受骗。马哈布·阿里说，他比其他所有的洋大人更愣头愣脑的。"

"呃！"吉姆说了一声便走了。傻瓜，他想没有人会把引发出动八千大军和大炮的情报告诉傻瓜。统帅军队的总司令不会，像吉姆听见的，跟傻瓜讲话。马哈布每每提到上校的名字都要改变声调——这其中必有蹊跷。

马哈布可能是在为上校刺探消息，正如吉姆为马哈布刺探消息一样。和马贩子一样，上校显然器重那种不卖弄聪明的人。

他庆幸没有泄露出他知道上校住在哪里；当他回到营房里，发现根本没有什么雪茄烟盒被落下时，他更是喜不自

rect person playing a hidden game. Well, if he could be a fool, so could Kim.

Father Victor took him to the station, and put him into an empty second class next to Colonel Creighton's first, Then he bade him farewell with real feelings.

"They'll make a man of you at St. Xavier's O'Hara — a white man — and I hope — a good man. The Colonel will look after you. When they ask your religion, remember to say that you are a Catholic."

He considered his own life — he was an unimportant person in all this roaring whirl of India, going he knew not to what fate.

Presently, the Colonel sent for him, and talked for a long time.

"Yes, and you must learn to make pictures of roads, mountains and rivers — carry them in your eye till a suitable time comes to set them down upon paper. Perhaps, you will be a chairman, I may say when we are working together — 'Go across the hills and see what lies beyond.' And you can bring me answers. There is a good spirit in you. Do not let it be blunted at St. Xaviers."

Several times in the long twenty-four hour journey, did the

胜。这是个完全符合他的心意的人——一个耍阴谋诡计的人。得，他能傻，吉姆也能。

维克多神甫把他带到火车站，让他坐进一节没有乘客的二等车厢，隔壁就是克莱顿上校的头等车厢，然后依依不舍跟他道别。

"在圣查维尔学校，欧哈拉，他们会把你培养成一个男子汉的——一个白人血统的男子汉，我希望，还是一个出色的男子汉。上校会照顾你，记住，他们问起你的宗教信仰，你就说是天主教徒。"

他思考着自己的生活，在印度这整片的喧嚣混乱中，他微乎其微，迈向前途未卜的明天。

不多久，上校派人叫他过去，跟他谈了好久。

"对了，你必须学会怎么把道路啊，山脉啊，河流啊画出来。先把这些看在眼里，等到适当的时候再把他们画到纸上。也许有一天——那时你当了测绘员，我们又在一起工作了，我会对你说，'翻过那几座山，去看看那边都有些什么。'而你会给我回答。你内心有一种锐气，不要在圣查维尔泯灭了这种锐气。"

在二十四小时的旅途中，上校派人把吉姆叫来好几次，

Colonel send for Kim, always developing this plan for him.

"We are all on one rope, then," thought Kim, "the Colonel, Mahabub Ali, and I — when I become a chairman. He will use me as Mahbub Ali used me. That is good, if it allows me to return to the road again."

When they came to the crowded Lucknow Station, there was no sign of the Lama. He swallowed his disappointment, as the Colonel bundled him into a horse-drawn carriage, and sent him alone to St. Xavier's.

"I do not say farewell, because we shall meet again," he said, "again, and many times, if you are one of the good spirits. But you are not yet tested."

"Not when I brought you a white stallion's pedigree that night?"

"Much is gained by forgetting, little brother," said the Colonel with a sharp look that pierced through Kim's shoulder blades.

It took him nearly five minutes to recover.

每次都阐发这个问题。

"这么看来，我们是同路人，"吉姆心想，"上校，马哈布，还有我——等我成了测绘员。他也会像马哈布以前用我那样的这样用我。那也不错，如果这能让我重新上路。"

当他们到达拥挤的勒克瑙火车站时，没有看见喇嘛的影子。吉姆大失所望，却隐忍不露，上校把他塞进了一辆马车，打发他独自前往圣查维尔学校。

"我不道别了，因为我们还会见面的，"他大声说，"还会见面，见很多次面，只要你还保持锐气。不过你还没有接受考验呢。"
"那天晚上我给你送去白种马的血统证明不算考验吗？"

"遗忘就能多受益，小兄弟。"上校的目光几乎穿透他的肩胛骨。

将近五分钟以后吉姆才恢复过来。

9

THE LAMA AT THE GATES
OF LEARNING

Kim sniffed the new air appreciatively. "A rich city," he said, "richer than Lahore." He made the coachman drive around for two hours before he told the driver to go to St. Xavier's.

It was growing dark, as they neared the gates, his eye caught a figure near the wall.

Kim raced on the road and touched the dusty feet of the Lama.

"I have waited here a day and a half," said the Lama.
"I came from Benares in the train, where I knew a man in the Tirthankara temple. He is a seeker like me."
"Ah! your river," said Kim. "I had forgotten the river."
"So soon, my chela, I have never forgotten it."
"But what are you doing now?"

九

学习之门前面的喇嘛

吉姆表示欣赏地呼吸着清新的空气。"一个富得流油的城市，"他说，"比拉合尔还富。"在告诉车夫去圣查维尔学校之前，他让车夫驾着车在城内四处转悠了两个小时。

当他们走近城门时，天色渐渐暗了下来。他被墙边的一个人影吸引住了。

吉姆跳到马路上，拍打喇嘛沾满尘土的双脚。

"我在这里等了一天半。"喇嘛说道。
"我从贝纳勒斯坐火车来，我认识那里特丹卡寺的一个人，他跟我一样，也是个寻求者。"
"对了！你那条河，"吉姆说，"我都忘了那条河。"
"这么快就忘了，我的弟子？我可不曾忘过。"
"可你现在做些什么事呢？"

"I acquire merit by helping you. I sent the money to help you for one year. Now I have come to see you go into the gates of learning. I have waited for a day and a half — not because of any affection for you — that is no part of the way, but because money having been sent, it was right that I should oversee the end of the matter."

"I am alone in this land. My heart was in that letter I sent you. Except for Mahbub Ali, who is a Pathan, I have no friend, except you, O Holy One. Do not go away altogether."

"I have considered that also," said the Lama in a shaking voice. "I will assume myself that your feet are set on wisdom. That way I shall gain merit."

"From time to time I will come to see you. May be you will be such a Sahib as one who gave me these spectacles in the Wonder House at Lahore." The Lama wiped his glasses carefully. "Again, may be you will forget me and our meetings."

"If I eat your bread," cried Kim passionately, "how shall I ever forget you?"

"No, no," he put the boy aside, "I must go back to Benares. Now that I know the custom of letter-writers, from time to time I will send you a letter, and from time to time I will come and see you."

"But where will I send my letters?" *Wailed* Kim, clutching the Lama's robe.

"To the Temple of Tirthankaras at Benares. Do not weep. If you love me then go up to the Gates of Learning for my heart cracks — I will come again. Surely, I will come again."

"我在行善积德，因为我帮助你，我把够一年用的钱寄去，现在我就来了，来看着你走进学问之门。我等了一天半，并不是因为我喜欢你，那与修道无关，而是钱已花了，我理当监督这件事有个结果。"

"我在这世上孤零零的一个人，我的心就在寄给你的那封信里了。除了马哈布·阿里，他是个帕坦人，还有你，圣者，我就没有朋友了。别走得远远的。"

"这事我也想过，"喇嘛声音颤抖着答道，"我能想象你掌握了智慧，立于其上。我通过那种方式来行善积德。"

"我会不时来看看你。你也许会成为像拉合尔的珍奇馆里那位给我这副眼镜的洋大人那样的人，"喇嘛仔细地擦拭着那副眼镜，"再说，也许你会忘记我，忘记我们的几次见面。"

"要是我吃你给的面包，"吉姆动情地哭泣道，"我怎么会把你给忘了呢？"

"不会的——不会的，"他没理会孩子，"我必须回贝纳勒斯。现在我知道这地方有人代写信件，我会不时写信给你，我还会来看你。"

"可是我给你的信要寄到哪里呢？"吉姆呜咽着，抓住僧袍。

"寄往贝纳勒斯的特丹卡寺。别哭了，你爱我的话，就走向学问之门吧，不然我会伤心的……我还会来，我一定会再来的。"

"The Gates of Learning" shut with a clang.

The country born and bred boy began to learn what the English masters taught. He suffered the usual punishments for breaking rules, but that was before he learned to write fair English, and needed a letter-writer. He rejoiced in the new found comforts and learnt self control.

"One must never forget that one is a Sahib. When the examinations are passed, one will command natives." Kim made a note of this, for he began to understand where examinations led.

Then came the holidays from August to October — long holidays imposed by the heat and the rains. Kim was informed that he would go north to some hill station beyond Umballa. Father Victor would make all the arrangements.

When Kim learnt that he would be sent to a barrack school, he considered it in every light. A boy's holiday was his own property, and now he could write.

He had two rupees and seven annas. With that he went out in the warm rain, snailing, and looked for a certain house whose outside he had noted down sometime before.

Kim had himself dyed brown, and waited till the colour dried. He paid four annas for it and ran out looking like a low-caste Hindu boy — perfect in every detail. Then he went to a cookshop and feasted extravagantly.

"学问之门"哐当一声关上了。

这个土生土长的孩子开始学习英国教员教的内容。由于违反规定，他遭受了不寻常的惩罚。在他还没有学会写像样的英语之前，他只得找代人写信的人。他在新发现的安慰中变得开心，也学会了自我控制。

"必须记住你是个洋大人，当各门考试均获通过后，你就要驾驭土族人。"吉姆领悟了这一点。他开始明白考试的意义何在。

接着八月至十月的假期到了——这是在炎热多雨的季节里安排的长假。吉姆得到通知，让他北上，到乌姆巴拉山区外的某个英军驻地，有维克多神甫为他安排好一切。

自从吉姆知道他将被派去营地学校，他每天晚上都想着这件事。孩子的假期就是他自己的财产。现在他学会写字了。

他有两个卢比七安纳。他走到屋外，在和暖的雨中微笑，然后朝一座他早些时候已经注意到外观的房子走去。

他把自己染成亚麻色，一直等它干了。他付了四个安纳，跑出来时看起来像是个低种姓的印度孩子——每个细枝末节都惟妙惟肖。接着他上了一家菜馆，美美吃了一顿。

At the Lucknow station he entered the third class compartment. That night Kim's happiness was beyond description.

About this time Colonel Creighton was in Simla, and he was informed by a telegram that young O'Hara had disappeared. Mahbub Ali was in town, and to him the Colonel gave the information. "Oh, that is nothing," said the horse-dealer. "He has gone back to the road again for a while. The school tired him. I knew it would. Do not be troubled, Sahib. It is as if a polo-pony has broken free, and run out to learn the game alone."

Next morning on the same course, Mahbub Ali's stallion rode up to the Colonel's side.

"It is as I had thought," said Mahbub. "Has come through Umballa, and learning I was here, has written a letter."

"The Friend of All the World has taken leave to go to his own places. He will come back on the appointed day. Let the box and bedding-roll be sent for. If there has been a fault let the hand of friendship turn aside the whip of *calamity*."

"See how weired he is. He has gone back to the Road again, as I said. Not knowing yet your trade, he turns to me to make peace between you and him. He says he will return, perfecting his knowledge. For my part, I am happy. The pony is learning his game."

在勒克瑙的火车站，他进了一节三等车厢，那天晚上吉姆快活得无法形容。

与此同时，克莱顿上校在西姆拉收到了电报，告知他小欧哈拉失踪了。马哈布·阿里也在那边。上校向他透露了这件事。"哦，那没什么，"马贩子说，"他又回到大路上去转会儿。学校让他腻烦了。我知道会这样的。别担心，克莱顿大人。就像是一匹打马球的小马，跑出去自己独自学玩游戏。"

第二天早晨，在同一个赛马场上，马哈布的种马和上校的并驾齐驱。

"果然不出我所料，"马贩子说，"他来到乌姆巴拉，打听到我在这里，就给我写了一封信。"

人尽可友告辞去他想去的地方。他会在指定的日子返回。请派人去取衣箱和铺盖；如果犯下了错误，请伸出友谊之手挡开灾祸之鞭。

"看看这孩子多聪明。像我说过的，他重回大路上。他还不知道你是干哪一行的，他找我帮忙，要跟你和解。他说他会回去增长见识。就我来说，我很高兴。小马在学着玩游戏呢。"

"It is true, Mahbub Ali. If he comes to no harm, I desire nothing better."

"He does not tell me where he is going. He is no fool. When the time is ripe, he will come to me. He ripens too quickly."

A month later Mahbub had gone down to Umballa to bring a fresh batch of horses. He met Kim on Kalka Road at dusk, riding alone, and begged *alms* of him. Mahbub swore at him, and he replied in English. There was nobody around to hear Mahbub's gasp of amazement.

"Who! Where have you been?"

"Up and down — down and up."

"Come under a tree, out of the wet, and tell me."

Kim told him how he had spent his holidays, and it pleased Mahabub Ali. "Shabash!" said Mabhub Ali.

"But what does the Colonel Sahib say? I do not wish to be beaten."

"The hand of friendship has turned aside the whip of calamity; but another time, when you take the road, you will come with me. This is too early."

"Late enough for me. I have learned to read and write English."

"Well are you tired of the road? Will you come on to Umballa with me and the horses?

"对，此话不假，马哈布·阿里。只要他平安无事，我就心满意足了。"

"他连上哪里去都没告诉我，他不再是个傻瓜，当时机成熟时，他就回来找我。他长得很快。"

一个月后，马哈布南下到乌姆巴拉去调运新到的马匹。黄昏时分，在卡尔卡大道上，他碰见吉姆独自骑着马向他乞求布施，马哈布责骂他，他用英语应答。边上没有人听到马哈布的惊叫。

"呵！你去哪里了？"

"从北到南——从南到北。"

"这里淋雨，到树下来吧，跟我说说。"

吉姆同他讲了他的假期经历，这使马哈布很开心。"真棒！"他说。

"可是上校大人怎么说呢？我可不想挨打。"

"友谊之手已经挡开了灾祸之鞭；不过下一次，你要再上路，那就得跟着我，你太年轻了。"

"不小了，我在学校里学会了用英语读读写写。"

"好了，你在路上逛腻了吗，想不想跟我到乌姆巴拉把那些马送回去？"

"I will come with you, Mahbub Ali."

On the road together, Mahbub Ali explained the importance of going back to school.

"You must learn distances and numbers, and how to use the compass. It is important for the game."

"I will learn their teaching on one condition," said Kim, "that my time is given to me when the school is shut. Ask the Colonel for this on my behalf."

"But why not ask the Colonel in his own tongue."

"The Colonel I have known for three months, and Mahbub Ali I have known for six years. So, I will go to school, and there learn to be a Sahib. But when the school is shut, I must be free to go among my own people. Otherwise I die!"

"And who are your people, Friend of All the World?"

"This great and beautiful land," said Kim, "and I would like to see my Lama again. And further, I need money."

"That is the need of everyone," said Mahbub Ali. "I will give you 8 annas, for not much money is picked out of horses' hooves. It must last you for many days. As to the rest, I am well-pleased. Learn quickly, and in three years, you will be an aid — even to me. Go and sleep among my men. You are my new horse-boy."

Mahbub felt in his belt, wetted his thumb on an ink-pad, and pressed the impression on the piece of paper. "Show this to the head man. I will come in the morning."

"我跟你去，马哈布·阿里。"

一起走在路上时，马哈布解释了重回学校的重要性。

"你必须要学好距离、数字，还有怎么使用罗盘，这在游戏里很重要。"

"我会学的，不过有个条件，"吉姆说，"学校里放假的时候，我的时间一定得归我自己。替我请求上校同意这个条件吧。"

"可是为什么不用洋大人的话向上校请求呢？"

"我认识上校不过三个月，可我认识马哈布·阿里已经有六年了。学校我是要去的，在学校里我会成为一个洋大人，可是学校放假的时候，让我回到我的人那里去，不然我宁可死掉！"

"可是谁是你的人呢，人尽可友啊？"

"就是这一片美丽的地方，"吉姆说，"我想见见我的喇嘛，还有，我需要钱。"

"这可是谁都需要的哦，"马哈布说，"我给你八安纳，因为卖马赚不了多少钱，可那也够你花上好几天的。至于其他的嘛，我很满意了。抓紧学习，三年以后，你就可以当助手了——我的助手。你现在是我的马夫。同我那些随从睡觉去。"

马哈布伸手在怀里摸索，大拇指往一锭墨上蘸了蘸，然后在一张纸上按下指纹："把这个拿给工头看就够了。我早上过去。"

10

KIM WARNS MAHBUB ALI

K im slid out quietly into the night and away from the station for a mile or so, and then went back at leisure.

Mahbub's men were camped on a piece of waste ground beside the railway. Mahbub's headman was *pacified* by the thumb signal and allowed Kim in who borrowed a blanket and curled up beside a horse-truck.

"Every month I become a little older," he thought sleepily. I was very young and a fool, when I took Mahbub's message to Umballa. I had no wisdom. Now I learn everyday, and in three years the Colonel will take me out of the school and let me go on the road with Mahbub hunting for horses' pedigrees. Maybe I shall find the Lama and go with him. Yes, that is best. To walk again as a chela with my Lama."

These thoughts came slowly and disconnectedly. He was slipping into a beautiful dreamland, when his ears caught a whisper, thin and sharp, coming from behind the horse-truck.

十

吉姆警告马哈布·阿里

　　吉姆不声不响地溜进夜色中。朝着离开车站的方向走了一英里左右。然后,慢悠悠地走回去。

　　马哈布的人马在铁路旁的一处荒地上扎营露宿,他的工头一看到马哈布的手印就变得和颜悦色,让他进来了。吉姆盖一床借来的毯子,在货车的轮子下蜷曲着躺了下来。

　　他昏昏沉沉地想着:"每过一个月我就长一岁。我把马哈布的密件送去乌姆巴拉时,我还很小,又傻乎乎的,没什么才智。现在,我每天都在学习,三年以后,上校就要把我从学校里接出来,让我跟着马哈布上路,去搜寻马的血统证明,也许我会找到喇嘛和他一起上路。对,那样最好,再当他的弟子和他一起走。"

　　他的思绪越来越慢,断断续续。他正要进入甜美的梦乡,突然听到一阵窃窃私语,声音又细又尖,从货车底下传出来。

"He is not here, then."

"He must not go back beyond the passes a second time. It is the order. There is a price upon his head."

"Then what is the plan? The police have a long arm."

"Wait till he comes to lie down, and then one sure shot. Then we'll run back over the lines. They will not see where the shot came from. Wait here at least till dawn. What manner of fakir are you to shiver merely watching it?"

"One," thought Kim. "They are looking for Mahbub again. A white stallion's pedigree is not a good thing to tell the Sahibs! Or maybe Mahbub has been selling other news. Now Kim, what to do? I do not know where Mahbub is housed, and if he comes here before dawn they will shoot him. It would not profit me, and it is not a matter for the police. I have not learned any lesson at Lucknow which will help me.(He almost laughed aloud.) First, Kim must wake and go away, so that they do not suspect me. A bad dream wakes a man thus — "

He threw off his blankets, and raised himself suddenly, making meaningless yells.

"Urr — urr — urr — urr! Ya — la — la — la — ! The churel! The churel!"

The churel is an evil ghost woman who has died in child-bed.

Louder rose Kim's howl, till he leaped to his feet and stag-

"这么说他不在这里了？"

"绝对不能让他再次溜过山口。这是命令。拿下他的人头可得赏金。"

"还能有什么打算，警察到处都是。"

"等他一回来躺下，就一枪把他干掉，然后我们掉头跑过铁路。他们看不见子弹从哪里打来。就待在这里至少等到天亮。你像个什么托钵僧，让你监视一会儿就直打哆嗦？"

"又一个，"吉姆想，"他们又在寻找马哈布了。白种马血统证明可不是好拿来卖给洋大人的！要不就是马哈布又在出卖什么情报了。现在怎么办呢，吉姆？我又不知道马哈布住在哪里，要是他天亮前回来，他们就会开枪打死他，那对我没什么好处，在勒克瑙学到的任何东西都派不上用场，（他几乎笑了）这事又不好报警，首先，吉姆得醒来然后离开，这样他们才不会怀疑。噩梦惊醒人——就这样了——"

他掀开毯子，突然放开嗓门，胡乱地喊着。

"呜——呜——呜——呜！呀——啦——啦——啦！媸茹姥！媸茹姥啊！"

媸茹姥是产妇死于分娩后变成的女妖。

吉姆的号叫声越来越大，最后他一跃而起，迷迷糊糊摇

gered off sleepily! While the camp cursed him for waking them up. Twenty yards further, he lay down again, taking care that the whisperers should hear his groans. After a few minutes he rolled towards the road and stole away into the thick darkness.

Two or three carts passed by, then a coughing policeman. Then came the sound of a horse's feet.

"Ah! This is more like Mahbub Ali," thought Kim.

"Mahbub Ali," he whispered. "be careful."

The horse was reined back. "They pick up all bones and nails in the city." He stopped to lift the horse's forefoot, bringing his head within a foot of Kim. "Down — keep down," he muttered. "The night is full of eyes."

"Two men wait for you to come behind the horse-truck. They will shoot you when you lay yourself, because there is a price upon your head."

"Did you see them? Was one dressed like a fakir?"

"I didn't see them. But one said to the other, 'What manner of fakir are you to shiver at merely watching it?'"

"Good. Go back to the camp and lie down. I will not die tonight."

Mahbub turned round his horse and disappeared. Kim raced back to his second resting place and recoiled himself in the blanket.

摇晃晃地走开了，整个宿营地都被吵醒了，响起一片叱骂声。他走了约莫有二十码又躺了下来，哼哼呀呀地，要让那些窃窃低语的人听见。几分钟后，他朝马路翻身一滚，溜进了漆黑的夜幕中。

两三辆马车过去了，然后是一个咳嗽的警察，接着传来一阵马蹄声。

"这很像马哈布。"吉姆想道。
"马哈布·阿里，"他低声说，"当心。"

那马被往后勒住。"他们把城里的骨头啊，钉子啊全挖出来了，"他弯下来抬起马的前蹄，这样一来他的头和吉姆的头相距不足一英尺。"头低下，别抬高，"他低声说，"夜里到处有眼睛。"

"货车后面有两个人等着你去。你一躺下，他们就要开枪打死你，因为有人出钱要你的脑袋。"

"你看到是谁了吗？是不是有一个穿得像托钵僧？"
"我没看见，不过有一个对另一个说，'你像个什么托钵僧，让你监视一会儿就直打哆嗦？'"
"很好，你回宿营地躺下。今晚我死不了。"

马哈布掉转马头消失了。吉姆往回跑，一直到他第二次躺下的那个地方，把自己裹入毯子。

"At least Mahbub knows," he thought contentedly. "I do not think those two men will profit by tonight's watch."

Kim tried his best to keep awake, but at the end of an hour was sleeping. Now and again a night train roared past within twenty feet of him, but it did not even weave a dream through his sleep.

Mahbub was anything but asleep. It annoyed him to know that people outside his tribe should want to kill him. His first and natural impulse was to catch them from behind and kill them. But then the police department would make a fuss.

Then a most brilliant idea came to him.

"By Allah, I will tell the truth to the English policemen. If they catch thieves, it is an honour for them." He tied up his horse outside the station, and strode on to the platform.

"Hullo, Mahbub Ali!" said a young police official. "What are you doing here? Selling horses?"

"No, I am troubled for my horses. I came to look for Lutuf Ullah. I have a truck load down the line. I saw two men crouching under the wheels of one of the trucks nearly all night. But fakirs do not steal horses, so I gave them no more thought. But I want to find my partner, Lutuf Ullah."

"And you didn't bother about it? It's just as well that I met you. What were they like?"

"They were only 'fakirs'. They may take a little grain from

"至少马哈布知道了,"他满足地想着,"我看那两人今晚算是白等了。"

吉姆竭尽全力想通宵醒着不睡,一个小时以后,他还是睡着了。夜班车不时沿着距他不到二十英尺的铁轨隆隆驶过,这甚至没能让他在睡眠中编织起一个梦来。

马哈布却彻夜未眠,想到那些外族人要谋杀他,他怒不可遏。他的第一个本能冲动是从后面拿下那两个人,把他们干掉。可那样的话,到时候警察局就会大惊小怪。

之后,他想到了一个绝妙的主意。

"真主在上,我这就去告诉警察。要是他们抓住了盗贼,还能立功受奖。"他把马拴在车站外面,然后迈开大步朝展台走去。

"你好,马哈布·阿里!"一个年轻的警官说,"你在这儿干什么呢?卖马吧?"

"不,我不在为卖马的事操心。我来找鲁特夫·乌利亚。我有一货车的马在铁路上。我看到有两个人差不多整个晚上一直趴在一辆货车的轮子下面。托钵僧是不偷马的,所以我也没多留心,我想找鲁特夫·乌利亚。"

"你没留意?真是的,让我碰上你了。他们长什么模样呢?"

"就是托钵僧嘛。他们也许就想从车上拿点米罢了。政

the many trucks up the line and the state would never miss it. But regards Lutuf Ullah — a tall man with a broken nose — ”

The officer had hurried off to wake up another keen policeman. Mahbub Ali laughed quietly in his *dyed* beard.

They will walk in their boots, making a noise, and then will wonder why there are no fakirs. Barton Sahib and the Young Sahib are clever boys.”

He waited a few minutes, expecting the two Sahibs hurrying up for action. A light engine slid through the station, and he caught a glimpse of young Barton in it.

“I judged him wrongly. He is not a fool,” said Mahbub Ali. “To take an engine to catch a thief is a new game.”

When Mahbub Ali returned to his camp at dawn, no one thought it *worthwhile* to tell him any news of the night. Only the new horse boy newly advanced to his service was called to Mahbub Ali’s tent to help in some packing.

“I saw it all,” he whispered. “Two Sahibs came on a train and fell upon the two men sitting under the truck, and struck them down, till they lay still as if dead. Then they put them on the train and I saw so much blood on the line. Come and see.”
“I have seen blood before. Jail is assured for them. What a tale! Now be swift with the saddlebags. We will take out the horses and go to Simla.”

府又不会丢失什么。说到鲁特夫·乌利亚嘛——高个儿，塌鼻子！"

那个年轻人已经急匆匆地跑去叫醒另一个热情高涨的年轻警察。马哈布·阿里透过那缕染色的胡子嗤嗤窃笑着。

"他们会穿着靴子，咔嚓咔嚓地走过去，然后他们会奇怪怎么不见什么托钵僧呢。他们都是聪明的小伙子——巴坦大人和杨格大人。"

他等了几分钟，等着看他们急急地准备行动。一辆不挂列车的机车一掠而过，他瞥见年轻的巴坦的身影。

"我刚才对那小伙子的评价错了，他还不完全是个傻瓜。"马哈布·阿里说，"坐上火车去抓小偷可是个新玩意儿。"

天亮的时候，马哈布·阿里来到了宿营地，没有人认为值得把夜间发生的事告诉他。除了一个刚被提升当小马夫的。马哈布把他叫进他的小帐篷里，让他帮忙打点行装。

"我全都知道，"吉姆说，"两个洋大人坐着火车过来。他们扑向坐在马车下的两个人，把他们撂倒，直到他俩像死人似的安静地躺着，然后我看见他们被带上火车。铁轨上有好多血呢，过来看看。"
"我之前看见过血，监狱他们是蹲定了。行了，快点收拾好鞍囊，我们把马拉出来，去西姆拉。"

Swiftly, the untidy camp broke up, and the horses were led along the Kalka road in the rain swept dawn.

Here Mahbub Ali told Kim that he was not wanted by Lurgan Sahib. He had to get training there, and it was an order.

"Men say, Lurgan Sahib does magic. Here begins the Great Game," said Mahbub Ali.

很快，乱糟糟的帐篷就被拆除了，他们在黎明雨后如洗的清新空气中牵着马上了卡尔卡大道。

此时，马哈布·阿里告诉吉姆勒甘大人没有找他，他不得不在那里接受训练，这是命令。

"人家说，勒甘大人会魔法，大游戏从这里开始了。"马哈布·阿里说。

11

AT LURGAN SAHIB'S HOUSE

Kim flung himself wholeheartedly into the new role. As soon as he reached the broad road, he saw a Hindu child.

"Where is Mr Lurgan's house?" demanded Kim.

"It is here," said Kim's guide, and halted in a verandah. There was no door, only a curtain of beads.
"He is come," said the boy, and vanished.

Kim felt sure that the boy had been posted as a guide for him. He boldly parted the curtains. A black-bearded man, with a green shade over his eyes was sitting at a table. One by one, he was picking up short, white flashing jewels and threading them on a silken string, and *hummed* to himself. The smells of sandalwood and jasmine oil caught his nostrils.

"I am here," said Kim.

十一

在勒甘大人的房子里

　　吉姆全身心地投入到新角色中。一上大道，他便看见了一个印度小孩。

　　"勒甘先生家在哪里？"吉姆询问道。

　　"到了。"吉姆的向导说着便停在一个走廊里。门敞开着，只拉上了一道珠帘。

　　"他来了。"那孩子说完，转身就不见了。

　　吉姆断定那孩子就是派来接他的，便壮着胆子掀开珠帘子。一个蓄黑胡子戴绿色遮光罩的男人坐在桌前，他正在一个接一个地拿起又亮又白的珠子穿在一根丝线上，嘴里还一边哼着。一股檀香，还有一丝令人难受的茉莉花油味扑面而来。

　　"我来了。"吉姆说。

He looked at Kim for a full half minute.

"Do not be afraid," said Lurgan Sahib suddenly.

"Why should I fear?"

"You will sleep here tonight, and stay with me till it is time to go to Lucknow. It is an order."

"It is an order," Kim repeated, "but where shall I sleep?"

"Here in this room," said Lurgan Sahib, and waved his hand to the darkness behind him.

"So be it," said Kim. "Now?"

He nodded and held the lamp above his head.

As the light fell over them, a collection of Tibetan devil dance masks leaped into view. There were horned masks, masks of terror and anger. In a corner was a Japanese warrior, all plumed and ready. But the sight of the Hindu boy who had guided him, sitting cross-legged under the table of pearls, interested Kim.

"I think that Lurgan Sahib wishes to make me afraid, and that little boy wishes to see it," he thought. Aloud he said, "This place is like a Wonder House. Where is my bed?"

Lurgan Sahib pointed to a native quilt in the corner beside some hateful masks, picked up his lamp and left the room dark.

This was no cheerful night, the room being full of voices

　　他对吉姆凝视了足足半分钟。

　　"别怕。"勒甘先生突然说。
　　"我为什么要怕？"
　　"今晚你就睡在这里，一直跟我住到你回勒克瑙的时候为止，这是命令。"
　　"这是命令，"吉姆跟着说了一遍，"可我睡哪里？"
　　"就睡这个房间。"勒甘大人挥手指向背后那片漆黑处。

　　"行，"吉姆说，"现在吗？"

　　他点点头，拿下头顶上方的灯。

　　周围露出一些西藏魔鬼舞面具——有带角的面具，狰狞的面具，还有凶神恶煞的面具。一处角落里有个日本武士，全副盔甲，准备待战。更令吉姆感兴趣的是瞥见刚才为他做向导的印度小孩，正盘腿坐在放珠子的桌子下面。

　　"我想勒甘大人是想让我害怕,那个小鬼是想看我害怕。"他想道。然后他大声说："像一个怪屋，我的床在哪儿？"

　　勒甘大人指了指那些面目可憎的面具旁的角落。随后他拿起灯走了，房间里顿时一片漆黑。

　　那一夜过得可真不舒服，房间里满是讲话声、音乐声。

and music. He stuffed his jacket into the mouth of the box, silenced it and slept peacefully.

In the morning he was aware of Lurgan Sahib looking down at him. The man held out a hand.

"Shake hands, O' Hara," he said.

Kim looked at him out of the corner of his eyes.

He seemed to understand what moved in Kim's mind before he opened his mouth.

More than the purely Persian meals cooked by Lurgan Sahib with his own hands, the shop fascinated Kim. The Lahore Museum was larger, but here there were more wonders — ghost daggers, prayer wheels from Tibet, necklaces and bangles, devil-masks and figures of Buddha. There were carpets and Persian water jugs, and arms of all kinds. There were silver belts and a thousand other odd things lay around a small table where Lurgan Sahib worked.

"Those things are nothing," said his host. "I buy them because I like them, and I sell them if I like the buyer's look. Some of my work is on the table."

It blazed in the morning light — all red, green and blue. Kim opened his eyes wide.

他用力将夹克衫塞进盒子的口里。呼呼声戛然而止，吉姆就安然入睡了。

第二天早上，他就感觉勒甘大人正俯视着他。他把手伸了过来。

"握手，欧哈拉。"他说。

吉姆用眼角打量着他。

在吉姆开口之前，他似乎已明白了吉姆在想什么。

比起勒甘大人亲手烹煮的纯波斯风味早点，这个店铺更让吉姆着迷。拉合尔博物馆虽然比较大，可这里古怪的东西更多些——西藏的镇鬼短剑、祈祷轮、项链、手镯、魔鬼面具和佛像。那里有地毯、波斯水罐和各式各样的武器。银色腰带和其他奇异的东西堆放在勒甘大人工作的小桌旁。

"那些东西一钱不值，"主人说，"我买来是因为我喜欢他们，有时也卖出——如果我看中买主的长相。桌上只是我一部分的作品。"

那堆宝石在晨光照耀下熠熠闪烁——清一色红、蓝、绿的闪光。吉姆睁大双眼。

He moved to the end of the verandah to refill the heavy, porous clay water-jug from the filter.

"Do you want to drink?"

Kim nodded. Lurgan Sahib, fifteen feet off, laid one hand on the jar. Next instant, it stood at Kim's elbow, full to within half an inch of the brim.

"Wah!" said Kim in amazement.
"This is magic." Lurgan Sahib smiled. "Throw it back," he said.
"It will break."
"I say, throw it back."

Kim threw it. The jar fell and broke into fifty pieces, and the water dripped through. "I said it would break," said Kim.

"Look at the largest piece."

Kim looked at it and saw a sparkle of water in it. Lurgan Sahib laid a hand gently on the nape of his neck, and *stroked* it twice or thrice, and whispered, "Look! It shall come to life again, piece by piece. Just the big piece will join itself with the two others. Look!"

To save his life, Kim could not have turned his head. The light touch was firm. His blood tingled. The jar had been

他走到暗廊尽头，拿着沉重的土制素烧瓷罐，在滤水池里装满水。

"要喝水吗？"

吉姆点点头。勒甘大人站在十五英尺以外，一只手放在水罐上。一眨眼水罐已落在吉姆肘边，罐里的水只差半寸就满罐口。

"哇！"吉姆惊诧不已。
"这是法术。"勒甘大人微微一笑，"把它扔回来。"他说。

"水罐会破的。"
"我说了，扔回来。"

吉姆扔过去，水罐就掉到地上，摔成五十块碎片，水往下渗。"我说过会破的。"吉姆说。

"看那块最大的碎片。"

吉姆看到积水闪烁着亮光，勒甘大人把手轻轻放在他的颈背上，抚摸两三下并低声说："看着，它会一片一片地起死回生，先是那块大的和左右两块连起来。看着！"

吉姆为了保住性命一直没敢转头。颈背上的触摸紧紧的，他周身血液沸腾。水罐明明就在他眼前打破了。勒甘

smashed before his eyes. A wave of prickling fire raced down his neck, as Lurgan Sahib moved his hand.

"Look, is it coming into shape?" whispered Lurgan Sahib. He had been muttering softly for the last minute.

"It is there as it was," said Kim.

"It is there as it was," said Lurgan, watching Kim closely.

"But it is smashed — smashed," gasped Lurgan Sahib.

"You are the first of many who has ever seen it so." He wiped his broad forehead.

"Was that magic?" asked Kim. The tingle had gone from his veins, and he felt unusually wide awake.

"Tell me, did you see the shape of the pot?"

"For a little time. It began to grow like a flower from the ground."

"And then what did you think?"

"Oah, I know it was broken, and so I thought — it was broken."

"Has anyone done that sort of magic before?"

"If they had," said Kim, "would I let you do it? I would have run away?"

"And now you are afraid — eh?"

"Not now."

Lurgan Sahib looked at him more closely than ever. "I am pleased with you. You are the first that ever saved himself. For a long time I have not met anyone worth teaching. There are ten days before you return to Lucknow. I think we shall be friends."

大人的手移动了一下，一股针刺般的热流从他颈部迅速往下涌动。

"你看，它逐渐成形了吗？"勒甘大人低声说。他一直在喃喃低语。

"它还是刚才的样子。"吉姆说。

"它还是刚才的样子。"勒甘紧盯着吉姆。

"可是它被打碎了——碎了。"吉姆气喘吁吁地说。

"看过这过程的人很多，你是第一个这样看的。"他擦拭着额头。

"那也是法术吗？"吉姆问。血管里的刺痛消失了；他感到异常清醒。

"告诉我，你刚才看到水罐的形状了吗？"

"有一阵子。它开始像花一样从地上长起来。"

"那时你怎么样？"

"噢，我知道它碎了，所以我想——它是碎的。"

"以前有人对你施过这种法术吗？"

"要是有，"吉姆说，"我会让你再这样做吗？我会逃走的。"

"现在你不怕了吗？"

"不怕。"

勒甘大人更认真地注视着他："我对你满意，你是第一个能保全自己性命的人。我已经很长时间没碰到一个值得教的人了，离你去勒克瑙还有十天的时间。我想我们会成为朋友。"

They were a most mad ten days, but Kim enjoyed himself too much to think about their craziness.

In the morning they played the memory game, with a variety of things — stones, swords, daggers and even photographs of natures.

Through the afternoon he and the Hindu boy would mount guard in the shop, sitting silently and watching Mr Lurgan's money and curious visitors. There were small Rajahs, escorts and ladies looking for necklaces, natives and Babus. Each one came for a specific reason.

At the end of the day, Kim and the Hindu boy were expected to give a detailed account of all that they had seen and heard — their view of each man's character, as shown in his face, talk, and manner, and their idea of his real *errand*.

After dinner, Lurgan Sahib turned to what might be called dressing up. Largan Sahib could paint faces marvellously, and change them beyond recognition. The shop was full of all kinds of clothes. Kim was dressed as a young Mohammedan, as the son of an Oudh landowner, an oilman. Mr Lurgan would explain how each caste behaved, talked, walked, spat or sneezed. Kim's heart sang with joy as he put on the different dresses and changed his speech and gestures accordingly.

那简直是疯狂的十天。可是吉姆过得快活极了，整天乐颠颠的。

早上他们用不同的东西玩记忆游戏——宝石、剑、匕首，有时甚至用照片。

下午他和印度小孩就一直在店里看守着，静静坐着，照看着勒甘先生的钱，注视着好奇的顾客。他们中有小王公及他们的随从；有选购项链的贵妇人；还有土著人和巴布①。每个人都怀着一种特定的原因来到这里。

每天晚上，吉姆和那个印度孩子必须详细叙述他们白天的所见所闻——他们依据每个人的脸部表情、言谈举止判断每个来客的性格特征以及他们对每位来客真实来意的看法。

晚饭后，勒甘大人的兴趣就转到被称为化装的游戏上。他画脸的功夫堪称一绝，可以使它们变得无法辨认。店铺里有各式各样的服装，吉姆曾被装扮成名门望族出身的穆斯林青年，有时是卖油郎。勒甘大人会解释不同的种姓怎样举止、讲话、走路，怎样吐痰或打喷嚏。换装时吉姆总是快活极了，依据服装的变换调整言谈举止。

---

①巴布：印度对男子的尊称。

One evening, in his enthusiasm, Kim showed Lurgan Sahib how the disciples of a certain caste of 'fakir' behaved, and what language he would use to an Englishman, a Punjabi farmer, or to a woman without a veil. Lurgan Sahib asked Kim to stay as he was for half an hour. At the end of that time, entered an *obese* Babu, and Kim began begging like a street side beggar.

Lurgan Sahib did not watch Kim's acting, but watched the Babu.

"I think," said the Babu heavily, "I am of the opinion that it is a most extraordinary and efficient performance. How soon can he become chain-man?"

"That is what he must learn at Lucknow."

"Then order him to be jolly-dam-quick. Good night, Lurgan," and the Babu walked out.

When they were talking over the day's list of visitors, Lurgan Sahib asked Kim who he thought the man might be.

"I — I think he will want me when I come from school but I do not understand — "

"You will understand many things later. He is a writer of tales for a certain Colonel. His name is Hurree Chunder Mookerjee."

"True. But the days go slowly for me. There are yet years and years before I can even be a chain-man."

有天晚上他来了兴致,向勒甘大人表演某个种姓的托钵僧的徒弟们怎样行乞,怎样用不同的语言对英国人、旁遮普人和不戴面纱的女人讲话。勒甘大人让吉姆保持这个姿势达半小时之久。半小时后,进来一个肥硕的印度绅士。吉姆像路边乞丐那样行乞。

勒甘大人转身看印度绅士,不再观看他的表演。

"我,"印度绅士慢条斯理地说,"依我看,表演逼真出色。他要多久才可以成为一个算得上胜任的测绘员呢?"

"那时他必须在勒克瑙学习的。"
"这样的话,该死的,命令他快点学。晚安,勒甘。"印度绅士走了出去。

当他们谈论当天的来访者时,勒甘大人让吉姆说说那个印度绅士的身份。

"我——我想我离开学校后他会要我,不过,我不明白——"

"以后你会明白很多事情的。他专门为某个上校写故事。他的名字叫哈利尔·昌德拉·穆克。"

"说得对。可我总觉得日子过得好慢。还得等好多年好多年以后我才能成为一个测绘员。"

"Have patience, Friend of All the World!" — Kim started at the title."You must go back to Lucknow, and be a good little boy. Perhaps, next holidays if you come back to me — "

Four days later, a seat was booked for Kim and he sat with his trunk at the rear of a Kalka tonga. His companion was the fat Babu, shivering and grunting in the morning chill.

"It was a heart-shaped box, with three compartments for *betel* nut, lime — and pan — leaf. But it was filled with little bottles. I am found of drugs, and they are *handy* to cure poor people too. These are good drugs — quinine and so on. I give it to you as a souvenir. Now good-bye. I have urgent business — here by the roadside."

He slipped out as noiselessly as a cat on Umballa road, hailing a rickshaw, while Kim sat tongue-tied with the brass betel-box in his hands.

"要有耐心，人尽可友！"对此称呼吉姆大吃一惊，"你必须回勒克瑙去，做个好孩子，也许下一个假期，你可以回到我这里来。"

四天以后，有人为吉姆预留了一个位置。吉姆和他的小箱子上了一辆驰往卡尔卡的双轮小马车的后座。他的旅伴就是那个胖胖的巴布，他在清晨的寒气中一边瑟瑟发抖一边咕咕哝哝。

"这是个心形盒子，里面分成三格，用来放槟榔、菩提果和蒌叶。现在却放满了小瓶子。我喜欢各种药物，用它们来治疗穷人也很方便。它们都是好药——金鸡纳霜等。我把它送给你做个纪念。好了，再见。我在这路边还有点要紧的事要办。"

他像猫一样悄无声息地溜下车，站到乌姆巴拉路上，然后招呼一辆单座小马车走了。吉姆张口结舌，手里摆弄着槟榔铜盒。

12

THE HOLIDAYS

Kim passed his examination in elementary surveying with credit at the age of fifteen years and eight months. From then on, against his name stood the words — "Removed on Appointment."

Kim knew better now than to leave Lucknow city in native dress. He first headed to Mahbub's camp, and made his change under the Pathan's careful eyes.

Mabhub had work in Quetta, so Kim worked for a fat sergeant for the time.

That was in the Monsoon holidays.

The Christmas Holidays he spent with Lurgan Sahib. The road had four feet of snow in that season. The Hindu had gone away to be married. Kim sat with Lurgan Sahib and was made to learn whole chapters of *Koran* by heart. Moreover, he taught Kim the names and properties of many

十二
假 期

吉姆以优异的成绩通过了勘测考试，那一年，他十五岁零八个月。从那时起，他的名字旁注明"另有任用予以除名。"

吉姆现在不再穿着土著服装离开勒克瑙。他先来到马哈布的住处，当着这个谨慎的帕坦人的面换装。

马哈布在奎达有事，因此当时吉姆便到一个胖子军人家中干活。

这是雨季假期里的事了。

圣诞节假期，他跟勒甘大人在一起度过，路上积了四英尺厚的雪。那个印度孩子办婚事去了。勒甘和吉姆坐在一起，他让吉姆一整章一整章地背读《古兰经》，他甚至还让吉姆认识很多土著药的名称和特征，以及它们的用法，还有

native drugs and how to use them, and how to take care of his own body — cure of fits, and simple remedies of the road.

A week before it was time to go, Colonel Creigthon Sahib sent him a written examination paper that concerned itself only with rods, chains, links and angles.

"This was unfair," thought Kim.

Next holidays, Kim was out with Mahbub, touring the city of Bikaner, plodding through the sand, Kim nearly died of thirst. It was not an amusing trip for Kim, for the Colonel had ordered him to make a map of that wild, walled city. Bikaner was the capital of an independent native state, so Kim could not use survey chains. He was forced to pace all his distances. He used the compass and the survey paint box and prepared his picture. Mahbub advised him to prepare a written report as well.

Then he translated it for the Pathan.

Mahbub was pleased and rewarded Kim with a 450 revolver.

Then sorrowfully, in European clothes, Kim went second class to St. Xavier's.

Three weeks later Colonel Creighton, pricing Tibetan ghost

怎样保重自己的身体，合适的治疗，以及一些路途中的简单疗法。

离开之前的一个星期,克莱顿上校大人寄给吉姆一份尽是关于测量杆、测链、连杆和角度的笔试考卷。

"这是不公平的。"吉姆想。

接下来的假期里，他和马哈布外出，他们艰难地穿过沙漠，来到比卡尼尔城，他差点渴死。对吉姆来说，这段旅程并不有趣，因为上校命令他绘制一幅那座有城墙、未开化的城市地图,这是个独立邦的首府。所以，吉姆不能用测链。他只好用脚步测出所有距离。他用罗盘和测绘盒绘制了一幅地图。马哈布劝他同时写一份书面报告。

然后他把报告翻译给这个帕坦人。

马哈布很开心地取出一把四五零左轮手枪,作为对吉姆的奖励。

吉姆忧伤地穿上欧式服装，坐在二等车厢里，回到圣查维尔学校去。

三个星期后,克莱顿上校来到勒甘大人店里为买卖几把

daggers at Lurgan's shop, faced Mahbub Ali, openly in great anger.

"The pony is made — finished — and paced, Sahib. Drop the reign on his back and let him go," said the horseman. "We need him."

The black-bearded Lurgan nodded in agreement. "I should have used him long ago," said he. "The younger the better. You sent him to me to try. I have tested him in every way, and find that he is the only boy I could not make to see things. I have taught him a good deal since, Colonel Creighton. I think you waste him."

Mahbub and Creighton both shook their heads. "Let him go with his Lama," said the horse-dealer. "He can learn his paces by the rosary. Besides he is fond of the old man."

"All right, let the boy run with the Lama for six months, then we will see. Hurree Babu can keep an eye on him."
"Will he draw pay?" asked the practical horse-dealer.
"Food and water allowance only, and twenty rupees a month."

Mahbub saw the credit coming to him from his pupil. Lurgan had, made him E. 23.

But the joy of these masters was pale beside the joy of Kim,

154

西藏魔鬼匕首讨价还价，马哈布·阿里公开与他针锋相对。

"小马驹已经长成——调教过，练过步法了，大人。松掉他背上的缰绳吧，让他闯去，"马贩子说，"我们需要他。"

黑胡子的勒甘表示同意地点了点头。"我早就该用他了，"勒甘说，"年纪越小越好。你送他到我这里来受试。我用了各种方式考验他：他是唯一不受我的法术迷惑的孩子。我教给他许多东西。克莱顿上校，我认为你这是在糟蹋他。"

马哈布和克莱顿连连摇头。"还是让他跟喇嘛吧，"马贩子说，"他喜欢那老头，可以用念珠计算脚步。"

"好吧，让那孩子跟着喇嘛云游六个月，然后我们见面。哈利尔·巴布可以照顾他。"
"给他工资吗？"务实的马贩子问。
"只有吃喝的津贴。每月二十卢比。"

马哈布看到由于他学生的出色表现，对他这个导师的美誉也源源而来。勒甘大人造就他成了今天的E.23。

可是这些导师的喜悦跟吉姆的喜悦相比简直微不足道。

when the St. Xavier's Head called him. "I understand O'Hara, that Colonel Creighton has found you a place as an assistant chain-man in the Canal Department. It is great luck for you, for you are only sixteen. You are not going out into the world to enjoy yourself. There is a great deal of hard work before you."

But Kim was busy thinking of Mahbub's letter for a meeting at a certain house.

They met and went up a filthy staircase that led to an upper chamber, that was warm and dark. "We will *fortify* you against the risks of the road. That is my gift to you, my son. Take off all metals on you and lay them here."

Kim dragged forth his compass, survey paint-box, and medicine-box.

A woman rose slowly, and moved with her hands a little spread before her. Then Kim saw that she was blind.

"The Pathan speaks the truth," she said, "my colour does not go in a week or a month. Those whom I protect are under a strong guard. I will give you full protection of the road."

He did not like the white sightless eyes. But Mahbub's hand on his neck-bowed him to the floor.

"Be still," he said. "No harm will come to you."

当圣查维尔学校的校长叫他的时候,吉姆欣喜若狂。"我知道,欧哈拉,克莱顿上校在运河部为你找到一份助理测绘员的工作。你是很幸运的,因为你只有十六岁。你到社会上不是去享受,你面临许多艰苦的工作。"

吉姆在忙着思考一封马哈布的来信,信里约他下午到一个房子见面。

他们见了面,爬上一个肮脏的楼梯,这楼梯通往一个又热又暗的房间。"我们要加强你的力量以防路上遭遇不测。这是我给你的礼物,我的孩子。把你身上的金属物全拿出来,放在这里。"

吉姆掏出罗盘、测绘用的颜料盒,还有药盒子。

那女人慢腾腾地站了起来,双手在前边稍微张开,吉姆这才发现她是个瞎子。

"帕坦人说的是实话,"她说,"我的染料在一周甚至一个月内都不会褪掉。经过我保佑的人都能得到强有力的防护。我要给你一路上全面的保护。"

吉姆不喜欢那双泛白的瞎眼。马哈布的手按住他的脖子,把他放倒在地上。

"别动,"他说,"没人会伤害你的。"

A match lit the darkness, and he smelt incense. Then the room filled with smoke and he felt drowsy. She touched him with horrible soft fingers, but Mahbub's grip never shifted, till at last he relaxed with a sigh, and became unconscious.

"That work is done. May the boy be better for it," said Huneefa, the blind woman.

Mabhub chuckled. "Now let us finish the colouring. The boy is well-protected."

In the early hours of the morning, when Kim woke up, he felt he had been sleeping for a thousand years. Huneefa snored heavily in her corner, but Mahbub was gone but Kim saw another face.

"I supervised the whole operation."
Kim recognised the voice of Hurree Babu.

"And I also have the honour to bring down from Lurgan Sahib, your present costume — this dress of chela attached to a lamaistic Lama. Complete in every particular. I will set you on your way to Benares," he said. "You can spend time with your Holy One. She has charmed you against all devils and dangers. It was Mahbub's wish."
"Now you must listen well," said Hurree Babu, when they were in the fresh air. "If you feel in your neck, you will find one small silver amulet. That is ours."

黑暗中一根火柴点亮了，他闻到一股香味。接着房间里香雾弥漫，他感到昏昏沉沉。她用可怕的手指摸摸按按，马哈布则始终紧按住他的脖子，直到后来那孩子舒了口气，昏睡过去。

"好了，大功告成！愿那孩子由此受益。"亨妮法——那个盲女人说。

马哈布轻声暗笑："上色就此结束吧，那孩子已经很好地保护起来了。"

清晨，当吉姆醒来时，他觉得自己好像已经沉睡了上千年。亨妮法在角落里鼾声大作。马哈布已经走了，可吉姆看到了另一张脸。

"我监视了整个过程。"
吉姆认出了哈利尔·巴布。

"我很荣幸地从勒甘先生那里带来了你现在要穿的服装，这是喇嘛教的随行弟子穿的普通衣服，应有尽有。我送你上路，去贝纳勒斯，"他说，"你可以和圣者在一起。她已经用法术保佑你不受一切魔鬼和危险的伤害。这是马哈布的心愿。"

"现在你好好听着，"当他们走到户外呼吸着新鲜空气时，哈利尔说，"你摸摸脖子，有一个小小的银护身符，那就是我们的。"

"Yes. I have a dilli (heart lifter)," said Kim, feeling his neck.

"Huneefa, makes them with all sorts of magic, only for us. We put in one small piece of *turquoise*, when we get them. Mr Lurgan gives them. Colonel Creighton does not know. Now, you may go with the Lama, with me, or with Mahbub. We do get into very tight places. You say , 'I am the Son of the Charm'. Now — 'Son of the Charm' means that you may be a member of the 'Sat Bhai' — The Seven Brothers — an extinct 'Tantric' society. The natives always stop to think before they kill a man who belongs to this organisation. But suppose, I come to you dressed quite different. You would not know me unless I choose. Suppose I come as trader from Ladakh — and say — 'You want to buy precious stones?' You say , 'Do I look like a man who buys precious stones?' Then I say, 'Even very man can try a turquoise or tarkeean.' "

"That means — 'vegetable curry'," said Kim.

"Of course it is. You say, 'Let me see the tarkeean.' Then I say, 'It was cooked by a woman, and perhaps it is bad for your caste.' Then you say, 'There is no caste where men go to — look for tarkeean.' You stop a little between those words — to — look. That is the whole secret. The little stop before the words." Kim repeated the test-sentence.

"That is alright. Then I will show you my turquoise if there is time, and you will know who I am. And we will give each other news and documents and all those things. So it is with

"真的，我有一个壮胆的玩意儿。"吉姆在脖子上摸索着说。

"那些驱邪除魔的玩意儿全是亨妮法做的。她只为我们做。拿到护身符之后，我们就往里面放一小块绿松石。勒甘先生给的，克莱顿上校对此一无所知。你可以跟着喇嘛，或者我，或是马哈布。当我们陷入一个该死的困境时，你就说'我是符咒之子'。现在'符咒之子'的意思就是说，你可能是七兄弟会的成员，这是印度密宗组织。当地人在他们杀掉这个组织的成员之前往往会犹豫一下。不过假如现在，我衣着与平常不同，来到你面前。除非我有意，否则你绝对认不出我。我装扮成拉达希商人，说，'你要买宝石吗？'你就回答，'我像个买宝石的人吗？'然后我说，'即使很穷的人也买得起绿松石或塔吉安。'"

"那表示咖喱蔬菜。"吉姆说。

"当然，没错。你说，'让我看看那个塔吉安。'然后我说，'它是由一个女人做的，可能对你的种姓不好。'你就说，'去——找塔吉安的人没有种姓之分。'你在'去'和'找'之间稍微停顿一下。这就是秘密所在——在两个字之间稍微停顿一下。"吉姆把这个句子重复讲了一遍。

"完全正确。要是有时间，我会让你看看我的绿松石，那你就知道我是谁了，然后我们交换意见、文件什么的。跟我们当中的任何人接头都是这样。眼下，你还没有什么正式工

any other of us. At present you have no official business. But if you are called upon — to help the sons of the charm — you jolly well try it. Now I shall say good-bye, my dear fellow, and hope, you will come out *topside* up all right. For now, the Lama expects you. Good-bye."

作，但是如果你被要求帮助符咒之子，你得快乐地去试试
看。咱们道别吧，亲爱的小伙子。祝你平安归来。因为喇嘛
在盼望着你，再见。"

13

WITH THE LAMA AGAIN

"Now I am alone — all alone," Kim thought! "If I die today, who shall bring the news — and to whom? If I live and God is good, there will be a price upon my head, for I am a son of the Charm — I, Kim," and passing his hand before his eyes, he shook his head.

"Go in hope, little brother," said a long-haired Hindu holy man. "It is a long road to the feet of the One — but towards it do we all travel."

Kim did not feel so lonely after this.

He found Benares a filthy city, but his clothes were very respected. He was guided to the Temple of the Tirthankaras, about a mile outside the city, near Sarnath, by a Punjabi farmer, whom he met by chance. This farmer had begged every god to cure his small son, and now was trying Benares as a last resort.

"Whom do you serve?" asked the farmer.

十三
再次和喇嘛在一起

"现在我是孤单一个人了——孤孤单单的，"吉姆想，"要是我今天死了，谁会把消息传出去，传给谁呢？要是我活着，又有老天保佑，就会有人悬赏要我的人头，因为我是符咒之子——我，吉姆。"他用手在眼前摆一摆，摇了摇头。

"带着希望去吧，小兄弟，"一个长发的印度圣僧说，"通往世尊足下的路长得很，可我们还是人人都要上路的。"

这之后吉姆不再感到那么孤单了。

贝纳勒斯城给他的第一个印象是肮脏得出奇，不过人们对他的僧袍很是恭敬。吉姆在一个他无意中碰到的旁遮普农民的引导下，来到城外约一英里处、靠近萨纳斯的特丹寺。那农民拜遍了所有神明，祈求治好他小儿子的病，最后来到贝纳勒斯试一试。

"你为谁服务？"农民问。

"A most holy man at the Temple of the Tirthankaras."

The child looked at Kim through heavy eyelids.

"And was it all worthless?" asked Kim with interest.
"All worthless — all worthless", said the child, lips cracking with fever.
"Many priests have dealt with me — but my son is my son — and if a gift to your master can cure him — I am at my wits end."

Kim thought, tingling with pride. The man had given him respect — that proved he was a man. Besides he had tasted fever once or twice already, and knew enough to recognise starvation when he saw it.

"I'll call him forth, and try that the child is cured."

Kim halted at the carved outer door of the temple. A man in white clothes asked him his purpose.

"I am a chela of Teshoo Lama, a Holy One from Tibet. He asked me to come. I am waiting. Tell him."

Kim's message was carried inside, and the old man rushed out.

Hardly had the tall figure shown in the doorway, when the

"特丹寺里的一位大圣僧。"

那孩子耷拉着困倦的眼睑望着吉姆。

"难道都没有用吗？"吉姆饶有兴趣地问。
"都没用——都没用。"那孩子说，嘴唇因发烧而裂开了。

"很多僧人都跟我打过交道，可我的儿子还是老样子，要是给你师父送点礼物能治好他——我真的是一点办法也没有了。"

吉姆想了一想，不禁自鸣得意起来。眼前这个人对他的尊敬说明他已经长大成人了。再说，他也尝过一两次发烧的滋味，一眼便可看出这病是饥饿引起的。

"我把他请出来，尽力把孩子的病治好。"

吉姆在寺庙的雕花大门前停下。一个身穿白衣的人问吉姆有什么事。

"我是来自西藏的德寿喇嘛的弟子。是他叫我来的。我在这里等，请告诉他。"

吉姆的口信带进了庙内。老人迎了出去。

喇嘛高高的身影刚在门口出现，那扎特人已冲到他面

Jat ran before him, and lifting up his son cried, "Look upon him, Holy One, if the Gods will, he lives — he lives," and drew out a silver coin from his belt.

"What is this?" The Lama's eyes turned to Kim.

"It is no more than a fever," said Kim. "The child is not well-fed." "If it be permitted, I may cure, Holy One."

"What have they made you a healer? Wait here," said the Lama, and sat down by the Jat, while Kim slowly opened the betel-box. Quinine he had in tablets, and dark brown meat pills — probably beef — but that was not his concern. The little one would not eat, but sucked the brown pills greedily, liking the salt taste.

"Take then these six," Kim handed them to the man. "Praise the gods and boil them in milk, other three in water. After he has drunk the milk, give him this — (it was half a quinine pill), and wrap him up warmly. Give him the water of the other three, and the other half of the white pill, when he wakes up. Meanwhile there is another brown medicine, he may suck on the way home."

"God's wisdom," said the man, snatching the medicines.

It was as much as Kim could remember of his own treatment in a bout of malaria.

"Now go! Come again in the morning."

"I will come tomorrow with the child, and the blessings of the Gods of the Homesteads be upon you both."

168

前，举起孩子喊道："圣者，瞧这孩子，如果神灵愿意，他就能活——他就能活！"他从腰带里掏出一枚小银币。

"这是怎么回事？"喇嘛转过身来看着吉姆。

"不过是发烧罢了，"吉姆说，"那孩子营养不够。要是您同意，我可以试着治治看，圣者。"

"是什么，让他们使你变成一个医师了。等一等，"喇嘛边说边靠着扎特人坐下。这时吉姆慢慢地打开那个小槟榔盒子。他有奎宁片和深褐色的肉片——可能是牛肉，但这不关他的事。那小家伙不吃，只是贪婪地吸吮肉片，他喜欢这咸咸的味道。

"那就把这六个药片拿去，"吉姆将药递过去，"赞美神灵吧。三片放在牛奶里煮；另外三片放在水里煮。喝完牛奶后给他这个（半粒奎宁片），把他盖暖和。睡醒后给他喝放了另外三片药煮的水加剩下的半粒白药片。这里还有一种褐色药可以让他回家路上吸吮。"

"神灵啊！多有智慧！"那人说着一把抓过药片。

吉姆对自己曾经治疗过一场秋季疟疾就记得这么多。

"现在走吧，明天早上再来。"

"我明天再带着孩子来，愿家乡的神明保佑——保佑你们俩。"

He moved away *crooning* and mumbling.

The Lama looked at Kim, and all the love of the old man's soul poured through the eyes.

"To heal the sick is to acquire merit, but first we must get knowledge. That was wisely done, Friend of All the World."

"I was made wise by you, Holy One," said Kim, forgetting the healing he had just done, forgetting St. Xavier's, forgetting his white blood, forgetting even the Great Game, as he stooped to touch his master's feet in the dust of the Jain Temple. "My teaching I owe to you. I have eaten your bread for three years. My time is finished. I have been set free from the school, and so come to you."

"Herein in my reward. Enter! Enter! And all is well." They passed to the inner courts of the temple, "stand that I may see. So! It is no longer a child, but a man, ripened in wisdom and walking like a healer. I did well when I gave you up to the soldiers on that black night. Are you freed from the schools? I would not have you unripe."

"I am all free. In due time I will take up service under the Government as a *scribe*."

"Not as a warrior. That is well."

"But first I have come to wander with you." He went on quickly. "Tell me about yourself."

The old man chuckled, "I make pictures of the Wheel of Life. It takes three days to make a picture."

170

他连哼带唱地走了。

喇嘛面朝吉姆，眼睛里流露出满腔慈爱之情。

"治病是行善积德；可是先要有学问。你做得对啊，人尽可友。"

"圣者，是你使我变聪明的，"吉姆边说边俯下身子，在特丹寺的地面上触摸师父的双脚时，他把那场刚刚结束的小把戏，连同圣查维尔学校，还有他的白人血统，甚至连"大游戏"全部置之脑后，"多亏了你，我才能进学校。我吃你给的面包已经三年了。我已经学成。我离开学校了。我找你来了。"

"这就是我得到的回报，进来！进来！一切都好吗？"他们走进内院，"站好了，让我看看。不再是个孩子，而是个大人了。聪慧灵敏，走起路来像个医生。在那个漆黑的夜里，把你让给那些带枪的士兵时，我做得真对。你完成学业了，我可不要你半途而废。"

"完成了，时间一到，我就在政府部门当抄写员。"

"不是当士兵，那很好。"

"不过我要先同你一起去漫游，"吉姆说得很快，"说说你自己吧。"

老人扑哧一笑："我画轮回图，三天画一幅。"

He drew from under the table a sheet of scented yellow Chinese paper, brushes, and a slab of Indian ink. In clean outline he had traced the Great Wheel with its six *spokes*, and where they joined at the centre — were — pig, snake and dove — (symbols of ignorance, anger, and desire). The compartments of the Wheel were all the heavens and hells, and all the chances of human life.Men said that the Bodhisat first drew it with grains of rice to teach his disciples the cause of things, with every line carrying a meaning. Few can translate the meaning of the pictures. There are not twenty in the world who can draw it without a copy. Those who can draw and explain it, are only three.

"I have learned a little to draw," said Kim. "But this is a wonder."

"I will teach you the art — and show you the meaning of the Wheel."

"Shall we take the road, then?"

"The road and our search. I was but waiting for you. It had been made plain to me in my dreams — that without you. I cannot find my river. I feared this was an *illusion*, so I waited till you finished your time at school. Together we will go out again, and our search is sure."

"Where shall we go?"

"How does it matter, Friend of All the World. Our search is assured. If need be, the river will break from the ground before us. We are together, and All things are as they were — Friend of all the World — Friend of the Stars — my chela."

他从桌子下面抽出一张有奇特香味的黄色的中国纸、几支画笔和一锭印度墨。他已经用最简洁的线条勾勒出六个轮辐。轮辐的中心是相连的猪、蛇和鸽（愚蠢、愤怒和贪欲），所有轮辐间隔都代表天界地狱和人生一切的机会。人们传说这幅画一开始是菩萨自己用谷粒在地上画的，用来向弟子揭示万物之因缘。每根线条都有意义。没有几个人能够阐释这种图画的寓意；能准确无误地把它默画出来的人全世界不到二十个；这其中能画又能解释的人则只有三个。

"我学过一点绘画，"吉姆说，"可这幅图确实妙不可言。"

"我会教你这门艺术，我还要把轮回的意义解释给你听。"

"然后我们就上路吗？"

"上路并开始我们的寻求。我专门在等你。每次梦里都示意得明明白白，没有你我就永远找不到我的圣河。我生怕这是个幻象。所以我一直等到你完成学业，我们又将再次一起云游，我们的探寻就有把握了。"

"我们到哪里去？"

"那有什么关系呢，人尽可友？我们的寻求是有把握的。必要的话，圣河会在我们面前从地里涌现。我们在一起，一切都和过去一样，人尽可友，星辰之友，我的弟子。"

14

THE WOUNDED PASSENGER

A couple of hours later, they piled into the train, and slept through the heat of the day. At Somna Road, there tumbled into the compartment, a mean little person — a Mahratta, as Kim could judge. His face was cut, his clothes badly torn, and one leg was bandaged. He told them that a bullock cart had overturned and nearly killed him, and he was going to Delhi where his son lived.

Kim watched him closely. If he had rolled over the earth, there should have been signs of gravel and dust. But all his injuries were clean cuts. A mere fall from a bullock cart could not cast a man into such an extreme state of terror. With trembling hands he knotted his torn cloth about his neck, laying bare an amulet, strung round his neck with a copper wire.

Pretending to scratch his bosom, Kim exposed his own amulet. The Mahratta's face changed.

十四

受伤的乘客

两三个小时后，他们都挤上了火车。在闷热的大白天他们一路昏睡。在索姆纳，一个又小又瘦的下等人跌跌撞撞地滚进车厢。吉姆判断出他是个马拉塔人。他的脸被割伤，上衣被撕碎，一只腿包着绷带。他告诉他们一辆乡下的大车翻车，差点要了他的命。他现在去德里，他儿子在那里。

吉姆仔细地打量着他。如果他在地上打了好几个滚的话，那么皮肤上应该有沙砾磨伤的痕迹。可他的伤口全是干净的伤口，而且仅仅翻车也不至于使一个人这般失魂落魄。当他用发抖的手指把脖子上的破布打成结时，露出了护身符，它用一根铜丝系着挂在脖子上。

吉姆装作要挠挠胸口，不经意地把自己的护身符也抓了出来。那马拉塔人脸色刷地变了。

"Yes," he went on, "I was in a hurry, and besides the harm done, I lost a full dish of 'tarkeean.' I was not the 'Son of a Charm' that day. That was a great loss," said the farmer and lost interest.

"Who cooked it?" said Kim.

"A woman," the Mahratta raised his eyes.

"But what about the caste?" said Kim.

"Oh, there is no caste where men go to — look for Tarkeean," replied the Mahratta, in the taught style. "In whose service are you?"

"The service of this Holy One." Kim pointed to the Lama.

"Ah, he was sent from the Heaven to aid me. Great is his wisdom. He is called a Friend of All the World, and also the Friend of All the Stars. He walks as a healer."

"And a Son of the Charm," said Kim under his breath.

"Are you a healer? I am in deep trouble," cried the Mahratta.

"Show me the cuts," Kim bent over the Mahratta's neck, his heart beating. This was the Great Game. "Now, tell me your story swiftly, brother, while I say a charm."

"I came from the South, where my work lay. One of us was slain lay on the roadside. Have you heard of it?"

Kim shook his head. He, of course knew nothing of the previous E.23, killed in the dress of an Arab trader.

"Having found the letter which I was sent to seek, I escaped from the city and ran to Mhow. There I found they

"是的，"他继续说，"我很匆忙，这不但害我受伤，还丢了一整盘的塔吉安。那天我不是个符咒之子（运气不好）。损失够大的。"农夫说着没了兴趣。

"谁煮的？"吉姆问。
"一个女人煮的。"马拉塔人睁大眼睛。
"不过是什么种姓呢？"吉姆说。
"噢，去——找塔吉安的人没有种姓之分，"马拉塔人按规定方式回答，"你伺候哪位？"

"我伺候这位圣者。"吉姆指着喇嘛说。
"嗬，他是上天派来帮助我的，他非常聪慧，他叫做人尽可友，也叫星辰之友。他走起路来像个医生。"

"还是个符咒之子。"吉姆悄声说。
"你是行医的吗？我可是焦头烂额了。"马拉塔人声音大起来。
"让我看看伤口，"吉姆弯下身察看马拉塔人的脖子，他的心狂跳不已，这是大游戏，"兄弟，我念咒时，你快讲讲经过。"
"我从南方来，我的工作在那里。我们的一个人在路边被杀。这事你听说了吗？"

吉姆摇摇头。他当然不知道 E.23 的前任被杀死时，一副阿拉伯人的打扮。

"我拿到了派我去找的一封信，就离开。我逃离那个城市，跑到冒城。在那里我发现他们正四处找我。我贿赂了警

were looking for me. So I ran from Mhow, bribing the police. I lay hidden in the city of old Chitor for a week, in a temple, but I could not get rid of the letter. I burried it under the Queen's stone, at Chitor, in a place known to us all."

Kim did not know the place, but he did not interrupt.

"I was hunted like a jackal, I heard there was a charge of murder against me in the city I had left. They had both — the dead body and the witnesses."

"But cannot the government protect you?"

"We of the Game cannot be protected. If we die, we die. That is all. I changed my face, and made myself a Mahratta, and came to Agra. I would have gone back to Chitor to recover the letter. I was sure that I had given everyone the slip, that I did not send a telegram to anyone saying where the letter lay. I wished to take all the credit."

Kim understood.

"But at Agra, a man stopped me in the streets. I ran and came on foot to Somna Road. I had only enough money for my ticket to Delhi. Here someone sprang out and beat me, and cut me, and searched me from head to foot."

"Why didn't he kill you?"

"They are not so foolish. I am marked — he touched the bandage on his leg, "so that they will know me in Delhi."

"You are safe in the train, at least."

察，逃出冒城。我在赤陀城里待了一个星期，藏在庙里。我不能放弃那封信。我就把它埋在赤陀城里的皇后石下面，那地方我们的人都知道。"

其实吉姆并不知道，但他并不会让关系中断。

"我被追得像条落水狗，又听说有人控告我在离开的那个城市杀了人，人证和物证俱在。"

"政府不能保护你吗？"
"我们参加游戏的是没人保护的。如果我们死了，也就死了。我化装打扮成马拉塔人，来到亚格拉，本想再回赤陀城去取信。我满以为已经把他们甩掉了，所以没有发电报说出藏信的地方。我想独占全部功劳。"

吉姆理解那种心情。

"可是在亚格拉大街上走的时候，有一个人把我拦住了，我挣脱出来，一路走到索姆纳，袋里的钱只够买张到德里的火车票。就在那里，猛地跳出一个人来，又是打，又是砍的，还把我从头到脚搜个遍。"
"他为什么不干脆把你杀了？"
"他们没那么傻，我被打上了标记——"他摸摸腿上的包扎，"所以在德里他们还会把我认出来的。"
"至少在火车上算是安全了。"

"Live a year in the Great Game and then tell me. Information regarding every tear and rag upon me has been sent to Delhi. They will raise twenty to a hundred witnesses."

Kim kept on examining in a doctor-like fashion, and thought out his plan in the meantime.

"Have you a charm to change my shape or else? or I am dead."

"Is he cured yet?" asked the farmer.

"No," said Kim. "He has to do penance, and sit in the clothes of a holy man for three days."

Kim took out flour, from the odd assortment of cloth, medicines, tobacco, curry powder etc.

"Quick! Be quick!" gasped the Mahratta. "The train may stop."

"A healing against the shadow of death." said Kim, and mixed the flour with charcoal and tobacco ash. E.23, silently slipped off his turban and let down his long hair.

"I see hope," said E. 23. "What's your scheme?"

"We must make you a Sadhu. *Strip*, strip swiftly," and he helped in tearing off the clothes. "Shake your hair over your eyes, while I scatter ash. Have a mark on your forehead," and used his survey paint-box. He marked his forehead, chest and legs with more ash.

"你先去干一年大游戏，再来跟我讲这话。有关于我的信息已被一丝不差地用电报发到德里去了。他们会让二十个人，甚至一百个人出来作证。"

吉姆在像一个医生一样继续检查的同时，想出了一个计划。

"你能用法术改变我的样子吗？不然我就死定了。"

"好了没有？"农夫问。
"还没有，"吉姆说，"他必须穿着圣僧的衣服静坐三天。"

吉姆从一堆七零八碎的东西中取出布块、药品、烟草、咖喱粉，等等。

"快，快点，火车快停了！"马拉塔人气喘吁吁地说。

"在死亡的阴影下治病救人。"吉姆边说边往面粉里加入煤炭和烟灰。E.23静静地拿下头巾，抖散黑色长发。

"我看有希望了，"E.23说，"你打算怎么办？"
"我们必须把你变成一个苦行僧。脱，快脱，"他帮忙脱衣服，"我撒灰的时候，你把头发抖散下来盖住眼睛。在额头上做一个标记。"他掏出勘测用的颜料盒，在他的额头、胸部和腿上抹了更多的灰。

"We must cover your legs and the cuts. Ash cures wounds," said Kim. "Give me that."

E.23 took a handful of opium pills from the tin box in the Jat's bundle and gulped them down. "They are good against hunger, fear and cold, and make the eyes red. Now I can play the Game. But what about my old clothes?"

Kim rolled them into a bundle and stuffed them into the loose folds of his tunic.

The Lama stared at Kim. "Friend of the Stars, you have gained great wisdom. Be careful it does not give birth to pride."

E. 23 released and in awed silence, they slid into Delhi in the evening, when it was getting dark.

A group of yellow trousered policemen followed a young Englishman.

"See the Sahib reading from a paper. My description is in his hand," said E.23. "They are going from carriage to carriage."

When they came to their compartment they saw the Lama deep in meditation and Kim *jeering* at the Sadhu for his drunkenness.

"我们得把你腿上的伤口盖住。灰还能治疗伤口。把那个给我。"吉姆说。

E.23 从扎特人的包袱中的一个锡盒子里面掏出了鸦片丸，吞了下去："它们对付饥饿啊寒冷啊都有效，又能让眼睛发红，现在我可以玩游戏了，可是这些旧衣服怎么办？"

吉姆把衣服卷成一捆塞入他僧袍的宽松皱绉里。

喇嘛盯着吉姆："星辰之友，你已获得大智慧。不过要注意，别因此滋生傲气。"

E.23 松了一口气，在充满敬畏的气氛中，他们于点灯时飞驰入德里。

一群身穿黄色裤子的警察跟在一个英国人后面。

"你看那个洋大人正在看一张纸，那上面就有我的长相，"E.23 说，"他们会把车厢挨个地搜查个遍。"

当那队人马来到他们车厢时，喇嘛在凝神默想，苦行僧喝醉了，吉姆在嘲笑他。

"Nothing here, but a group of holy men," said the Englishman loudly, and passed on.

"The trouble now," whispered E. 23, "lies in sending a
telegram about the place where I hid the letter, I was sent to
find. I cannot go to the telegraph office in this guise. Here
comes another Sahib!"

He was a tall superintendant of police, walking proudly,
twisting his moustache.

"I go to drink water," said E. 23. As he got out, he blun-
dered almost into the Englishman's arms.

"You drunk? You mustn't *lounge* about as though the Delhi
station belonged to you, my friend."

E. 23 answered with a stream of abuses.

"My good fool," The Englishman said. "Go back to your
carriage."

Slowly the Sadhu climbed back into the carriage, cursing
the D.S.P. by the curse of the Queen's stone, by the writing
under the Queen's stone — and by an *assortment* of Gods with
new names. "I don't know what you are saying," the Englishman said in anger, "but I know it's rude. Come out of that!"

E. 23 pretended to misunderstand, and produced his ticket,
which the English man snatched.

"这里什么也没有，除了一伙修道的。"英国人大声说着，继续往前走。

"现在的麻烦是，"E.23低声说，"要发个电报告诉他们我藏信的地方，那封派我去找的信。我这副样子不能去电报局。又来一个洋大人！"

这是个高个子，他捻着胡子大摇大摆地走来。

E.23说："我去喝点水。"他跌跌撞撞地冲出去，差点与那英国人撞个满怀。

"你喝醉了，我的朋友。你不能这样横冲直撞，好像整个德里车站全是你的似的。"

E.23出言不逊，破口大骂。

"可爱的傻瓜，"英国人说，"滚回你的车厢去！"

苦行僧慢慢地倒退着爬回车厢，诅咒着警察局长的子孙后代，皇后石啊，皇后石下面的信啊，还不时冒出一连串闻所未闻的神灵名字。"我听不懂你在说什么，"英国人生气地说，"但我知道那极端无理。你给我滚出来！"

E.23装成听错了，拿出车票，那英国人把车票一把夺了过去。

The Sadhu followed the policeman, and Kim slipped behind him.

"It is all right," whispered the Sadhu. "He has gone now to send word of the letter I hid. He has saved me from present difficulties, but I owe my life to you."

"Is he also one of us?"

"We are both fortunate. I will report to him of what you did for me. I am safe under his protection. We may work together at the game sometime. Farewell!"

Kim hurried back to his carriage, excited and confused for he didn't understand many things.

"I am only a beginner at the game, for sure," he felt.

那苦行僧跟在警察后面。吉姆则跟在他们后面溜了出来。

"没事了，"苦行僧低声说，"他现在去发电报，通知我藏信的地方。他救我逃脱了眼下的灾难，可是你救了我的命。"

"他也是我们的人吗？"

"我们俩都很幸运！我会向他回报你做的一切。有他的保护我就安全了。我们以后可能还会一起干的，再见。"

吉姆匆匆返回车上，他既兴奋又不解，因为很多事情他想都想不明白。

"我在游戏中刚起步，这一点是肯定的。"他想。

15

KIM'S EDUCATION WITH THE LAMA

"We will put these things behind us," said the Lama, "the jolting of the train — though a wonderful things has turned my bones to water. We will use clean air henceforward."

Often the Lama would make pictures of his text, or unfold the great yellow chart, bidding Kim — too ready — to note how the flesh took thousands of shapes — a slave to the pig, the dove or the serpent.

"I am answered," said Kim. "Can I ask a question?"

The Lama inclined his head.

"I ate your bread for three years. Holy One, from where did the — ?"

"There is much wealth in Tibet — as men call the wealth. In Tibet I have the illusion of honour. I ask for what I need."

十五

喇嘛对吉姆的教育

"我们把这些东西全丢开，"喇嘛说，"火车的颠簸是奇妙，它把我的骨头震得都化成水了。从现在起，我们要呼吸清新的空气。"

喇嘛常常拿这些画面作为他谈经说法的内容，或是摊开那张黄颜色的图表，叮嘱过分热心的吉姆注意，肉体的形状千变万化，奴隶会变成猪、鸽子或是蛇。

"我明白了，"吉姆说，"我能问一个问题吗？"

喇嘛点点头。

"我吃了你三年的饭，圣者。你来的那个地方——？"

"在西藏有很多财富——正如人们把它称做财富一样。在那里，我受尊敬。我需要什么就开口要。"

189

And he told stories of Tibet, speaking of Lhasa and the Dalai Lama, whom he had seen and adored.

So they enjoyed themselves, not overeating, not lying on high beds or wearing rich clothes. Their stomachs told them the time and people brought them food. The Lama was content with his disciple, and his mind turned more and more to his monastery, and his to the permanent snows.

News travels fast in India, and soon, an old Oriya servant, bearing a basket of fruits, begged them to honour his mistress with their presence.

"She is a virtuous woman," said the Lama, "but a great talker. Tell her we shall come."

They covered eleven miles in two days, and came to the Kulu woman's house. She held a fine tradition of hospitality, but age had not weakened her tongue or her memory. She paid compliments to Kim.

In the smoky evening, she sat behind loosely-drawn curtains and talked and talked.

"Now tell me of your comings and goings, and, Holy One, give me a charm against the most painful colics of my daughter's eldest son. Two years back, he gave me a powerful spell."

他讲起了西藏的故事，讲到拉萨，还有他见过的受敬重的达赖喇嘛。

师徒二人过得快活极了，不暴饮暴食，不享受锦衣高床。他们的肚子告诉他们时间的早晚，人们给他们吃的。喇嘛对他的徒弟感到很满意，他越来越多地想到他的寺院，还有永久的积雪。

在印度，消息总是不胫而走，一个年老的乌里亚仆人，手提一只竹篮——里面有很多水果，请求他们赏脸去见见他们的女主人。

"她是个好心人，"喇嘛说，"不过话太多了，告诉她我们会去的。"

他们在两天里赶了十一英里路，到了库鲁女人的家里，她盛情款待了他们。年龄增大并没有使她的舌头不灵或是记忆衰退。她对吉姆大加恭维。

到了傍晚，空中弥漫着炊烟，她就坐在微微拉开的轿帘后面聊了起来。

"现在把你来来去去的事讲给我听听。还有，圣者，我得向你要一个符治我女儿的大儿子的腹痛。两年前他给了我一道很灵验的符咒。"

While the woman talked to Kim, the Lama faded quietly to his room.

"Tomorrow when he sees my daughter's son, he will write charms, and can also judge the new 'hakims' medicines."

"Who is the 'hakim', Maharani?"

"A wanderer as you are, but a most sober Bengali from Dacca — a master of medicine. He relieved my suffering after eating meal by means of a pill. He travels selling excellent medicines. He even has papers, printed in English, of the cures he has made."

"Yes," said Kim. "His main trade is giving coloured water shamelessly, and taking money from kings and overfed Bengalis."

"Do not be jealous. Charms are better. See that the Holy One writes me a good amulet by the morning."

"Discussing medicine before the ignorant is like teaching the peacock to sing," said the hakim.

"True," said Kim.

Then the hakim's lips hardly moved as he shaped the words, "How do you do, Mister O'Hara? I am jolly glad to see you again."

Kim would not have been more astonished — he was not prepared for Hurree Babu here. It annoyed him that he had been fooled.

"Ah ha, I told you at Lucknow — I shall rise again and you shall not know me. How much did you bet?"

就在老妇人和吉姆聊天的时候,喇嘛悄悄地返回了自己的房间。

"明天他看到我女儿的孩子时,他就会画符的。他也可以评评那个新大夫的药。"

"那大夫是个什么人呢,女郡主?"

"一个达卡来的孟加拉人,和你们一样,是一个到处游荡的人——一个医药大师。我吃了饭以后胃不舒服,他给我一颗小药丸,一吃下去,病痛就缓解了。他到处卖他那些珍贵的制剂。他甚至还有一些纸张,印着英文字,说的是他怎么治好了别人的病。"

"是的,"吉姆说,"他们惯用的就是一些上了颜色的水,加上极端无耻。他们从那些君王和暴食的孟加拉人身上赚钱。"

"别嫉妒。符咒更有用,你得保证让圣者明早给我画个灵验的护身符。"

"在愚昧无知的人面前讨论医药无异于教孔雀唱歌。"大夫说。

"是的。"吉姆应和。

当大夫把一个个的词做成形状表达出来时,他的双唇几乎没怎么移动:"你好,欧哈拉先生! 非常高兴又见到你!"

吉姆惊讶极了,他一点儿都没想到会在这里遇到哈利尔·巴布。他因为自己被要弄而有些恼羞成怒。

"啊哈,在勒克瑙我就告诉过你,我会再露面的,到时你不会认出我来。嗯,你跟我打了多少赌?"

"But why come here, Babuji?"

"I came to congratulate you on your efficient performance in Delhi. He told me, I told Mr Lurgan, and he is pleased that you have done so well. All the department is pleased."

For the first time, Kim felt thrilled and proud with the departmental praise. But the Eastern training told him that the Babus do not travel so far just to compliment.

"Tell your tale, Babu," he said sternly. "Why are you here? Give me a straight answer."

"You are subordinate to me at present — departmentally, Mr O'Hara."

"I am not a child. I want to know," said Kim laughing, " if it is the game, I may help."

"Now you sit tight, Mr O'Hara — It concerns the pedigree of a white stallion."

"Still. That was finished long ago."

"When everyone is dead, the Great Game is finished. Not before. Listen to me till the end."

"可你为什么来这里呢，巴布吉？①"

"我来祝贺你在德里的非常出色的表现。他告诉了我，我又告诉了勒甘先生。勒甘先生很高兴，整个部门都很高兴。"

受到部门的称赞，吉姆有生以来第一次由于激动而感到无比自豪。不过他的东方心理告诉他，巴布不会为了传播颂词而四处漫游。

"巴布，说说怎么回事，"他厉声责令道，"你为什么会在这里？给我一个确切的答案。"

"按照目前的部门编制，你是我的下级，欧哈拉先生。"

"我不是三岁小孩了，我想知道，"吉姆笑道，"如果是游戏的事，我也许可以帮得上忙。"

"你坐好，欧哈拉先生。这是有关一匹白色种马的血统证明。"

"还是那回事？那早就结束了。"

"只有人全部死光了，大游戏才算结束，否则不会结束的。听我讲完。"

①巴布吉：印度人常在称呼和姓名后面加一个"吉"，以加重语气，表示尊敬和亲热，在对面交谈及演说时常用。

16

THE WHITE STALLION

Hurree Babu began the story. "There were five kings who prepared for a sudden war three years ago, when you were given the stallion's pedigree by Mahbub Ali. Our army fell upon them before they were ready, because of that news."

"Ay, eight thousand men with guns. I remember that night."

"But the government believed that they had learned their lesson, so the army was called back. It is not cheap to feed men in high hills. Two of the five Rajahs — Hila's and Bunar undertook to guard the passes against all coming from the North. A bond was made for so many rupees a month. At that time, I who had been selling tea in Leh, became an accounts clerk in the Army. When the troops were withdrawn, I was left behind to pay the coolies, who made new roads in the hills. This was part of the bond."

"So? And then?"

"I sent word that these two kings were sold to the North. Mahbub Ali, who was yet further North, confirmed it. The word was sent many times, but nothing was done. Only my

十六
白色种马

哈利尔·巴布开始娓娓道来："三年前有五个土王准备突然发动一场战争，就是马哈布·阿里给你那张血统证明的时候。因为得到了消息，我们的军队趁他们还没准备好先下手了。"

"噢，八千士兵带着枪炮。我记得那个晚上。"

"但政府以为那五个土王吸取了教训，便把军队撤走了。向高山关隘供应军用粮草费用很大。希拉斯和本纳尔——其中的两个土王答应守卫关隘，阻止北方入侵者。为了此项协约，政府每月支付大笔卢比。我原先一直在莱亚卖茶叶，那时就成了军队里的会计官。军队撤走以后，我留了下来，付酬劳给那些开山筑路的苦力。开山筑路包括在协约里。"

"是这么回事，那后来呢？"

"我三番五次送回消息，说这两个土王已被北方收买，马哈布·阿里那时在更北的地区，他也证实了这一点。可是

feet were frozen, and a toe dropped off. I sent a word that the roads for which I was paying were being made for the feet of strangers and enemies.

"This had become an open joke among the coolies. Then I was called to tell personally all I knew. Mahbub came there too.

"Now, that year, after the snow melting, came two strangers under the pretext of shooting wild goats. But they carried guns, chains and compasses."

"Oho! The thing gets clearer."

"They were well received by Hilas and Bunar. They made great promises and came as the agents of the Czar of Russia, bearing gifts. They went up the valleys and down the valleys, saying, 'Here is the place you can build a fort. Here you can hold the road against the army.' — the very roads for which I paid rupees monthly.

"The other three kings quickly informed the government of this — then came the order to me, 'Hurree Babu, go North and see what the strangers are doing.' I said to Creighton Sahib, 'We need no evidence.'"

"So you are going forth to follow the strangers?"

"No. To meet them. They are sportspersons, and are coming to Simla to send their horns and heads to be dressed.

"I shall get myself associated to their camp somehow — as an interpreter or some mentally weak or hungry person

政府没有采取任何行动。倒是我的双脚冻僵了，掉了一个脚指头。我送出消息，说由我付钱给苦力而修筑的路实际上是在替外来者和敌人修筑的。

"这在苦力当中已经是公开的笑话。后来，我被叫回去，把我所知道的作个口头报告。马哈布也回来了。

"结果是，那年雪化了以后，过来两个外国人，说是猎野山羊来的，可是他们带着枪、测链和罗盘。"

"呃，事情越来越清楚了。"

"他们受到希拉斯和本纳尔的盛情款待。他们作出种种保证，他们讲起话来像某个携带厚礼的大帝的代言人。他们在山谷里爬上爬下，指指点点，'这里可以搭一座堡垒。这里可以守住路口挡住大军。'——正是我每月付出卢比修筑的那些路呀。

"另外三个土王派人去告诉政府。然后才来了命令，'哈利尔·巴布，到北方去，看看这些外国人在干什么。'我对克莱顿大人说，'我们不需要证据。'"

"然后你就去跟踪那些外国人了？"

"不，是去迎见他们。他们正要来西姆拉，把猎到的兽角兽头送去制成标本。

"我得想办法打入他们的阵营，也许当翻译，或是一个精神委靡不振、忍饥挨饿的人。然后，设法收集所需情报。

and then pick up what I can. Only you see Mr O'Hara, I am unfortunately an Asian — and very fearful. I do not suppose that the two gentlemen will torture me, but I would like to keep assistance at I hand. This is an unofficial request. You can say, no."

"The end of the tale is true, but what about the beginning?"

"Oah! There is ever so much truth in it, and lots more than you can suppose," said Hurree sincerely. "You are coming — eh? I am going straight to Doon from here. It is a beautiful, green countryside. Then by Rampur to Chini. That is the only way. I want to walk with them to Simla. You see one Russian is a French man, and I know my French pretty well."

"He will be happy to go to the hills. If we can go together — "

"Oah! We can be quite strangers on the road. I can be four or five miles ahead. There is no hurry for Hurree — a European *pun*. You think till morning — it is near morning now," and without another word, lumbered off to his sleeping place.

Kim slept little. "Well is the Game called Great! — Truly it runs through all Hind. And my share and joy — I owe to the Lama — also to Mahbub Ali — also to Creighton Sahib, but chiefly to the Holy One. And I am Kim — Kim — alone in the middle of it."

"What was the result of last night's discussions?" asked the Lama.

只是你知道，欧哈拉先生，不幸的是，我是个亚洲人，再说，我又是个胆小鬼。我猜想这两个绅士不会用酷刑对付我，我希望在紧急情况下能得到帮助。这纯粹是个非正式的请求，你可以说'我不干'。"

"故事的结尾嘛，讲了真话，可前面那一部分呢？"

"噢，那当然是真的。实际上比你猜想到的还要多，"哈利尔一本正经，"噢，你来吗？我从这里直接去杜恩，那是景色优美、满目苍翠的乡间。再从兰普尔进入秦尼山谷，只能走那条路。我要和他们一块儿走到西姆拉。你知道，其中的一个俄国人实际上是个法国人，而我的法语相当好。"

"他肯定会很高兴能在山峦中行走。要是我们一块儿走的话——"

"呃，我们在一路上可以毫不相干。我走在你们前头，拉开四五里。哈利尔用不着哈利。①这是个欧洲双关语。你明早答复我。现在，都快早晨了。"他一句客套话也没说就慢腾腾地走往他的下榻处。

吉姆几乎没睡。"难怪叫大游戏！真的，它在整个印度来回穿梭。我也有份，玩得开心。都亏了喇嘛，也亏了马哈布·阿里，还有克莱顿大人，主要还是圣者。我是吉姆——吉姆——孤单一个人在这一切当中。"

"昨晚争吵的结果如何？"喇嘛问。

---

①意思是哈利尔用不着着急。因为 Hurree(哈利尔)与 hurry(匆忙)发音相似，所以是双关语。

"Oh, he is a strolling seller of drugs in the plains," said Kim. "In the hills there are fewer."

"Oh, the hills, and the snow upon the hills," said the Lama.

"They are very close." Kim thrust open the door and looked at the long, peaceful line of the Himalayas, shining in the morning sunlight.

The Lama sniffed the air sadly — longingly .

"If we go North," Kim questioned the morning sunrise, "Would not much of the midday heat be avoided by walking among the lower hills, at least?"

At noon the Babu strapped his drug box, took his gay blue and white umbrella and set off northwards to the Doon.

"We'll go in the cool of the evening, chela," said the Lama. "The good doctor told me that the people in the lower hills are religious and very generous — and they need a teacher."

"I am refreshed," said the Lama. "When we reach the hills, I may yet be stronger. The hakim spoke truly when he said a breath from the snows blows away twenty years. He is full of learning and in no way proud. I told him about a certain dizziness that rose from the back of my neck at night. He told me it rose from excessive heat — and would he cooled by air. I had not thought of such a simple remedy."

"Did you tell him of your search?"

"Assuredly. I told him of our dream. He said it would break

202

"噢，他是平原上一个走江湖卖膏药的，"吉姆说，"山区里这样的人不是很多。"

"啊，山区，还有山上的雪。"喇嘛说。

"它们很近了。"吉姆推开门，眺望着连绵不绝、宁静温和的喜马拉雅山脉，它在朝霞映照下闪闪发亮。

喇嘛如饥似渴地大口吸着来风。

"如果我们往北，"吉姆面对着冉冉上升的旭日，"在丘陵地带走，不是至少可以避开中午的大部分的酷热吗？"

中午，巴布背起他的药箱，手拿一把艳丽的蓝白两色的伞，朝北去杜恩的方向出发了。

"我们等到傍晚凉爽些再走，弟子，"喇嘛说，"那医生告诉我说，丘陵地带的人都很虔诚，很慷慨，而且他们需要一个教师。"

"我的精神完全恢复了，"喇嘛说，"等我们到了丘陵地带，我会更强壮的。那个大夫说雪山吹来的风能使人年轻十岁，他说得对极了。那大夫一肚子学问，可是他一点儿也不骄傲。我跟他讲，每到晚上我总觉得颈背上阵阵昏眩，他说这是酷热引起的，只有冷空气能治好。我怎么就没有想到这么一个简单的疗法。"

"你有没有告诉他你寻找的事？"

"的确，我把我的梦讲给他听了，他说，河会像我梦见

forth, even as I dreamed — at my feet, if need be. I have seen your prophecy accomplished. I was the instrument. Now you shall find my river, being the instrument in return. The search is sure."

He set his face, calm and untroubled, towards the inviting hills, his shadow falling far before him in the dust.

"Who goes to the hills, goes to his mother."

They crossed the Siwaliks and left Doon and Mussorie behind them. Day after day, as they struck deeper into the mountains, Kim watched the Lama return to the strength of a man. He breathed deeply the air of the mountains, and walked as only a hill man can. But being born and bred on the plains, Kim ached all over, sweated and panted.

"This is like my country," said the Lama.

At a height of nine or ten thousand feet, the winds became sharp and bit and these knife-edged breezes cut the years off the Lama's shoulders. "These are but the lower hills, chela. True cold will not come till we reach the true hills."

Except for a grey eagle or some brightly coloured birds, the Lama and Kim were alone in their walks with the winds and the grass. They often meditated upon the Wheel of Life. In the evenings they often *encountered* the doctor, but there were secret talks apart in the woods between the Babu and Kim. The doctor would seek herbs and Kim would accompany him.

的那样涌现出来——必要的话就在我的脚边涌现出来。我已经看到了你的预言的实现。我是它实现的助力。现在你要帮我找到我的河,我们的寻找肯定会有收获的。"

他面朝充满诱惑的高山,脸庞安详宁静,他的身影长长地投在他前方的地面上。

"到群山去就是回到母亲的怀抱。"

他们穿越了西瓦里克丘陵,把杜恩和莫苏里抛在脑后。他们一天天深入群山之中,吉姆也一天天看着喇嘛逐渐恢复体力。他深深吸了一口清新的空气,然后像山里人一样走了起来。平原生平原长的吉姆,挥汗如雨,气喘吁吁,一路上苦不堪言。

"这里像我的家乡。"喇嘛说。

当爬上九千或一万英尺的高度时,那些风变成了刺骨寒风。利如刀刃的寒风使喇嘛年轻了许多。"这些不过是小山,弟子。只有到了真正的高山,那里才算得上寒冷。"

除了灰色的老鹰,还有一些色彩艳丽的鸟儿之外,只有风和草同师徒俩人做伴。他们经常对着轮回转生图静思冥想。晚上,他们经常遇见那位医生。当吉姆作为徒弟伴随医生到密林深处采摘草药时,他们就谈起一些秘密的话题。

"You see, Mr O'Hara, I do not know what I shall do when I find our *sporting* friends. But if you will kindly keep within sight of my umbrella. I shall feel much better."

Kim looked across the jungle of peaks. "This is not my country, hakim."

"O, that is my strong point. There is no hurry for Hurree. They were at Leh not so long ago, and were coming down with their heads and horns and all. I am only afraid they may have sent back all their letters and things that may prove their guilt from Leh to Russia. Of course, now they will walk away as far East as possible — just to show they were never among the Western States.

"By the process of elimination and by asking the people I cure, I have ascertained their path. You will see me catch them somewhere in Chini Valley. Please keep your eyes on my umbrella."

They crossed the snowy pass in cold moonlight. They dipped across beds of light snow, and took refuge from a gale in a camp of Tibetans.

As usual the Lama led Kim through a cow-track and by road, far from the main route along which Hurree Babu had rolled along, three days before.

"欧哈拉先生，我真不知道发现了我们的游戏伙伴后，我该怎么办。当然，如果你能跟着我的伞，那我就放心多了。"

吉姆朝外望着重山叠岭："我不是在这里长大的，大夫。"

"哈，那可是我的拿手好戏，哈利尔用不着哈利。他们不久前还在莱亚呢。下来时，带了兽头兽角，应有尽有。我只是怕他们会把所有信件和能证明他们有罪的东西都从莱亚寄回俄罗斯去。当然了，他们现在会尽量朝东部走——以表明他们根本没有到过西部各邦。

"通过排除法，还有向我治愈的病人询问，我已经确定了他们的路线。你会看到我在秦尼山谷一带追上他们。请你一定要跟紧我的伞。"

在清冷的月光下，他们穿过一个覆雪的山口。他们深一脚浅一脚地走过了浅雪层，他们在西藏人的帐篷里躲过了一场飓风。

和往常一样，喇嘛又带着吉姆在远离大路的羊肠小道和岔道上行走。三天前，哈利尔·巴布就在大道上独自赶路。

17

THE MEETING

Hurree Babu had searched the huge valley with a pair of cheap binoculars. He saw all he wanted. Twenty miles away as the eagle flies, and forty by road, two small dots were seen just below the snow — line, and the next day had moved downward, about six inches on the hillside. Hurree Babu had seen all he wanted.

His fat bare legs could cover a surprising amount of ground. While Kim and the Lama had taken refuge against the storm, Hurree Babu reached his sporting friends. He put on his patent-leather shoes, and opened his blue and white umbrella with a beating heart. "What can I do for you, gentlemen?"

The gentlemen were pleased. Their native servants had become sick at Leh. They hurried, anxious to bring their spoils of the hunt before they were moth-eaten. Their coolies refused after a thunderstorm split a pine, to move forward, even when threatened with a rifle. So they welcomed the help of Hurree Babu, the agent for His Royal Highness, the Rajah of Rampur.

十七

会 面

哈利尔借助一只廉价双筒望远镜把偌大一个山谷上上下下搜了个遍。在离鹰飞处二十英里，大路四十英里的地方，他发现了他想找的目标——雪线下的两个小圆点，第二天在山腰间往下移动了六英寸。

他那双裸露的胖腿可以走很长的路程，所以，当吉姆和喇嘛还在躲暴风雪时，哈利尔·巴布已经赶上了他在游戏中的朋友。他穿上漆皮鞋，撑起蓝白相间的伞。惴惴不安地问："先生，请问，我可以为你们效劳吗？"

两位先生喜出望外。他们的土著仆人在莱亚病倒了。他们急于把猎物带走，以免被虫蛀掉。在暴风雨将一棵松树劈成两半后，他们的苦力都拒绝前行，即使是用莱福枪胁迫他们也不顶事。所以，他们对哈利尔·巴布——蓝姆普殿下的代理人的帮助表示欢迎。

One was clearly a Frenchman, while the other, a Russian, who spoke English like the Babu's. The Babu salaamed, and brought out the hiding coolies and three hangers-on, and after a three minute talk and promise of some silver, convinced them.

"My royal master will be much annoyed." said the Babu, "if your honours would kindly forget the unfortunate affair, I shall be much pleased. In a little while the rain will stop, and we can proceed. You have been shooting? That is a fine performance!"

He skipped nimbly from basket to basket, as if adjusting them, and accidentally upset one with a red oil skin top, and was struck across the wrist. He was given a glass of drink and he apparently came under its effect — talked of his dissatisfaction and Bengali love-songs, collapsing off to sleep, while they talked.

"We do not have time. We must get to Simla as soon as possible," said one.

The other answered, "I wish our reports had been sent back from Hilas or even Leh."

"The English post is better and safer. Remember, we have been given all the facilities. It is unbelievable stupidity."

"It is their pride that deserves punishment."

Hurree Babu, snoring loudly understood their talk and wished to cut their throats.

其中的一个很显然是法国人，而另外一个则是俄国人，他所说的英语和巴布讲得差不多，巴布等来了躲躲藏藏的苦力以及三个随从。经过了之后三分钟的交谈，答应给他们一些硬币，他们相信了。

"我的王爷主人会很恼火，"巴布说，"如果大人宽大为怀，不计较这件不幸的事，我将不胜欢喜。过一会儿等雨停了，我们就可以上路。你们一路打猎过来的，是吗？战绩辉煌啊！"

他轻快地从一只背篮跑到另一只背篮，好像是在整理。偶尔不小心把一只盖有红色油布的背篮打翻，他们也不至于大打出手。他们给他一杯饮料，他显然喝醉了，谈论着自己的不满，哼唱着孟加拉情歌，喋喋不休、摇摇晃晃地去睡觉了。

"我们可没有时间。我们必须尽快赶到西姆拉。"其中的一个说。

他的同伴回答："我倒希望我们在希拉斯，或者还在莱亚的时候就把报告寄出去了。"

"英国邮政既快又安全。别忘了我们可是得到一切便利的。他们真是愚蠢透顶！"

"那叫骄傲自大——自食其果，也是罪有应得！"

哈利尔·巴布在他们谈话时呼呼地大口喘着气，真想拧断他们的脖子。

Next morning they followed the Babu down the slopes, ahead of the coolies. Hurree's thoughts were many and various. The Sahibs travelled without servants — decidedly they were poor and ignorant for they believed a Bengali who appeared from nowhere.

"Decidedly this fellow is an original," said the taller of the two.

Under the striped umbrella Hurree Babu was keenly trying to follow the quickly spoken French, and keeping both his eyes on the basket with the maps and documents — an extra large one with a double red oil-skin cover. He did not wish to steal anything, but judge what to steal, and how to get away when he had stolen it. He thanked all the Gods, that there remained some valuables to steal.

The striped umbrella had been sighted by Kim, who suggested a halt till it came upon them.

On the second day, the Babu with his party reached them about sunset, and saw a Lama, sitting cross-legged and explaining a mysterious chart to a young disciple. "Ha!" said Hurree Babu. "That is an important holy man. Probably a subject of my master."

"What is he doing? It is very strange."
"He is explaining the holy picture all hand made!"

第二天早晨，他们跟着巴布走向山坡，走在苦力的前面。哈利尔心事重重。这两个洋大人没带随从，看来他们是穷洋大人，也没有多少见识，因为他们会相信一个不知来自哪里的孟加拉人的意见。

"这家伙绝对是个怪物。"个子较高的人说。

在条文图案的伞下，哈利尔·巴布正拉长耳朵集中精力跟上连珠炮似的法语，一边目不转睛地注视着一只放满地图文件的背篮——盖着双层红色油布，特别大的一只篮子。他并不想偷盗。他只是想知道有什么可偷的，偷了之后怎么溜掉。他感谢了众神，因为那里还有一些有价值的东西可偷。

吉姆看到了那把条文图案的的伞，于是他建议停一下。

巴布和他的团队在第二天日落时分赶上了他们。他们看见一位喇嘛盘腿而坐，他正在向一个年轻的弟子解释一幅神秘的图表。"哈！"哈利尔·巴布说，"那是很重要的一位圣人。多半是我王爷的臣民。"

"他这是在干什么呢？挺奇怪的。"
"他在解释圣画，那全是手工绘制的。"

The two men stood bareheaded in the afternoon sunlight, while the *sullen* coolies were glad to rest, and slid off their loads.

"Look," said the Frenchman, "it is like a picture for the birth of a religion."

The Babu advanced with his back to the two people, and winked at Kim.

"Holy One, these are Sahibs. My medicines cured one of them, and I am going to Simla to oversee his recovery."
"They wish to see your picture — "
"To heal the sick is always good. This is the Wheel of Life."
"They want you to explain it."
"This is an excellent way of doing good. Do they have any knowledge of Hindi?"
"A little, may be."

The Lama threw back his head and began with an *invocation*, before he started on his explanation. The strangers listened, and Kim watched their faces, while the coolies mutely crouched about twenty yards away in reverence. Only the Babu stood happily.

"These are the men," he whispered, "and all their books are in the large basket with the red oil skin top — and I have

两个人没戴帽子，沐浴在午后斜阳里。那些苦力很高兴有机会歇一歇，把背篮放下。

"你看，"法国人说，"这像是某种宗教诞生的一幅图画。"

巴布背朝着两位大人走上前去，同时朝吉姆眨眨眼。

"圣者啊，这两位是洋大人。我的药治好了他们中的一位，我要到西姆拉去关照他的恢复过程。"
"他们想看看您的画——"
"医治病人是善行。这是轮回转生图。"

"他们还想听您解释。"
"这是行善的最好途径。他们对印度有什么了解吗？"

"也许，有点吧。"

喇嘛把头朝后一扬，在开始解释前，他先做了祈祷。两个异邦人听着，吉姆则看着他们的脸。那些苦力噤若寒蝉，蹲在二十或三十码开外的地方。只有巴布开心地站着。

"就是这两个，"他低声地说，"他们的书全在那个红盖子的大背篮里，我还看见一封郡王的信，要么是希拉斯，要

seen the king's letter that either Hila's or Burnar has written. They guard it carefully. Nothing has been sent back from Hila's or Leh. That is sure."

"Who is with them?"

"Only hired coolies. They have no servants. They cook their own meals. Wait and see. Only if any chance comes to me, you will know where to look for the papers."

"That is enough," said one of the Sahibs. "I cannot understand him, but I want that picture. He is a better artist than I am. Ask him if will sell it."

"He said, 'No, sir,'" the Babu replied.

The Lama was an artist and a wealthy Abbot in Tibet.

"Perhaps in three or four days or even ten, if I find that the Sahib is a seeker, I may draw him another. But this is for teaching my disciple. Tell him so, hakim."

"He wishes it now, for money."

The Lama shook his head and began to fold up the chart. The Russian saw no more than an old man haggling over a piece of paper. He drew out a handful of rupees and half jestingly snatched the chart, which tore in the Lama's grip. A low murmur of horror went up from the coolies, some of whom were Buddhists.

The Lama rose at the insult, his hand going to the heavy iron pen case, that is the priest's weapon, and the Babu danced in agony.

么是本纳尔写的。他们看得特别紧。他们还没从希拉斯或莱亚寄回什么。这一点已经确定。"

"谁跟他们在一块？"

"只有雇用的苦力。他们没带仆人。他们连饭都自己烧。等着见机行事。只要我一有机会，你得知道上哪里找那些材料。"

"够了，"其中的一位王爷说，"我听不懂他说些什么，不过我想要那幅图。他画得比我们强。问他卖不卖。"

"他说，'不卖，先生。'"巴布回答。

喇嘛是个艺术家，在西藏还是个富裕的住持。

"说不定三天以后，或许四天，或许十天，如果我看出这个洋大人是个寻求者，我可能会画一幅给他。可这一幅是用来启蒙弟子用的。告诉他，大夫。"
"他现在就要——给钱的。"

喇嘛摇摇头，开始折起那幅图。在那个俄罗斯人看来，这不就是个老头子在就一张纸讨价还价嘛。他掏出半把卢比，半开玩笑地去抢那幅图，图在喇嘛手里被撕破了。挑夫那头发出了一阵恐怖的低声怨语——他们中有些是佛教徒。

喇嘛受此侮辱一下站了起来，他抓起沉重的铁笔盒，那是教徒的武器，而巴布则急得乱跳。

"Now you see, why I wanted witnesses. O Sir! Sir! You must not hit a holy man."

"Chela! He has *defiled* the written word!"

It was too late, the Russian hit the Lama full on the face. Next instant he was rolling over downhill with Kim at his throat.

The Lama dropped to his knees, half stunned, the coolies fled with their loads uphill, as fast as they could.

They had seen a crime against religion and desired to run away before the Gods and the devils of the hills took revenge. The Frenchman ran towards the Lama with his revolver, but the shower of stones from the hillmen drove him away. A coolie from Ao-chung pulled the Lama away. All came about as swiftly, as the sudden mountain darkness.

"现在你们知道了吧——为什么我要见证人。啊！先生！先生！你们可不能打圣人啊！"

"弟子，他亵渎了圣物！"

可是来不及了。俄罗斯人已经一拳打在老人脸上。接着吉姆掐住俄罗斯人的脖子一起滚下山坡。

喇嘛倒在地上，半昏过去。苦力挑着胆子往山上飞快跑去。

他们目睹了有悖宗教信仰的恶行，他们得赶在山里的众神和魔鬼报复之前逃走。那个法国人拔出手枪朝喇嘛跑去。可是山里人一阵急雨般的砾石把他赶跑了，一个坳昌的挑夫把喇嘛拉走了。这一切都在转瞬间发生，就像山里的夜色突然降临了一样。

18

THE BAGGAGE AND THE LAMA

"They have taken the baggage and all the guns," yelled the Frenchman, firing blindly into the twilight. "All right, sir, don't shoot! I go to rescue," said Hurree, running downhill to where Kim was banging his foe's head against a boulder.

"Go back to the coolies," he whispered. "They have the baggage. The papers are in the basket with the red top. Take the papers, and specially the King's letter. Go! The other man comes."

Kim tore uphill, as a bullet rang on the rock by his side.
"If you shoot," shouted Hurree, "they will come down and destroy us. I have rescued the gentleman, sir. This was particularly dangerous."

Kim touched the revolver (Mahbub's gift) in his bosom. He had never used it — but now pulled the trigger.

十八

行李和喇嘛

"他们把行李和枪全都抢走了，"法国人大声嚷嚷，一边朝暮色里一阵乱射。"行了，先生！别开枪。我这就去夺回来。"哈利尔跑下山去，到了吉姆那里，他正抓住他对手的头往石块上敲。

"回到挑夫那边，"巴布低语，"行李都在他们那儿。文件放在红盖子的背篮里。文件要收起来，特别是郡王那封信。快走。另外两个来了！"

吉姆飞奔上山。一颗子弹打在身旁一块石头上。
"你再开枪，"哈利尔大喊，"他们会跑下山来把我们全打死的。我已经救出了你的同伴，先生。情形很危险啊！"

吉姆摸着怀里马哈布送给他的礼物——一把枪。他从未用过这玩意儿，可现在他扣动了扳机。

"What did I say, sir."

The shots ceased. Kim hurried through the darkness to the Lama.

"Did they wound you, chela?" asked the Lama.

"No. And you?" and dived into a clump of fir trees. "Come we will go with these folk to Shamlegh under the snow."

"But not before we have done justice," a voice cried. "I have got all the four guns of the Sahib's. Let us go down."

"He struck the Holy One. We saw it! Our cattle will be barren — likewise our women too," said another.

The panic-stricken coolies could do anything in terror. "Wait Holy One," said the man from Ao-chung. "They cannot have gone far. Wait till I return."

For a moment the Lama hesitated. Then he rose to his feet, and laid a finger on the man's shoulder.

"I say there shall be no killing,"the Lama leaned on Kim's shoulder. "I have come near to great evil, chela," he whispered, and slid to the ground, breathing heavily.

"Have they hurt him to death?" said the man from Ao-chung. Kim knelt over the body in deadly fear. "No, this is only weakness. Open the baskets. The Sahibs may have some medicines."

"我不是说了吗，先生？"

枪声停了，吉姆赶紧趁黑跑到喇嘛那里。

"他们伤了你了吗，弟子？"喇嘛问。

"没有。你呢？"他一头钻进低矮的冷杉丛里，"走吧，我们跟着这些人到雪山下面的山姆里格去。"

"可我们先得讨回公道，"有人喊着，"洋人们四把枪全在我这里。我们下山去。"

"是他打了圣人。我们都看到的。我们的牲口不会产崽了，我们的女人也不会生孩子了。"另一个说。

挑夫们惊恐万状，他们惊恐起来可是什么事都干得出来。坳昌来的那个挑夫说："在这等一会儿，圣者，他们不会走太远的。等我回来。"

喇嘛犹豫了一会儿。然后他站起来，一个手指搭在那人肩上。

"我说不许杀人，"喇嘛靠在吉姆的肩上，"我差点做了大坏事，弟子。"他低声细语，瘫倒在地，呼吸沉重。

"那些人把他弄死了吗？"坳昌挑夫说。吉姆吓得跪倒扑在喇嘛身上："不，只是一阵虚弱。打开背篮，那些洋人可能有药。"

The Lama coughed and sat up, groping for his rosary.

"There shall be no killing," he murmured. "Just is the wheel."

"No, Holy One. We are all here," the Ao-chung man touched his feet. "Rest a while. Later, as the moon rises, we shall go to Shamlegh — under the Snow."

"There is a dizziness and pain at the back of my neck. Let me lay my head on your lap, chela. I am an old man, but not free from passion. We must think of the cause of things."

"Give him a blanket; we dare not light a fire."

"We will go to Shamlegh when the moon rises. There we will fairly divide the baggage between us. Then we will all go our ways, remembering that we have never seen or taken the service with these Sahibs," said the man from Ao-chung.

"These are not true Sahibs. All their skins and heads were bought in the bazaar at Leh," said the Ao-chung man. "We are not doing any wrong. They are priest-beaters, and frightened us. We fled! Who knows where we dropped the baggage?"

"What about the big basket with the red top that Sahibs packed themselves every morning?"

"Nothing — it is full of written word — books and papers, and strange instruments of worship. What we do not want we shall throw on Shamlegh Midden."

"The old man is still asleep. We will ask his chela."

"We have here," the Ao-chung man whispered to Kim, "a strange basket, whose nature we do not know."

"But I do," said Kim. "It is a basket with the red top and

喇嘛一边咳嗽，一边坐了起来，摸索着念珠。

"不能杀人，"他喃喃低语，"这是轮回之道。"

"没有杀人，圣者。我们全在这里呢，"坳昌挑夫拍着喇嘛的双脚，"歇一歇吧，回头等月亮升起来，我们去雪山下的山姆里格。"

"脖子后面好像有点晕。让我把头靠在你的腿上吧，弟子。我年纪大了，但有时还是会冲动，凡事都必须想到因果啊！"

"给他一条毯子，我们不敢生火。"

"月亮一升起来我们就到山姆里格去。在那里我们再来平分这些背篮。然后我们各走各的，要记得我们从没见过那些洋人，也没有帮过他们。"坳昌来的挑夫说。

"他们不是真正的洋人，他们那些兽皮兽头全是在莱亚的街市上买的，"坳昌来的挑夫说，"我们没有做错，他们打了僧人，还吓唬我们。我们这才逃走的！谁知道我们什么时候丢下行李的？"

"那只大背篮，那只红盖子的，每天早上洋人都要自己装的那只篮子呢？"

"没什么，不过塞满了经书和纸张，还有一些奇怪的东西，好像是礼拜用的。我们不需要的东西统统扔到山姆里格贝家里。"

"老人家还在睡。我们问问他的弟子吧。"

"我们这里有，"坳昌来的挑夫轻声地说，"有一只奇怪的篮子，不知里面是什么名堂。"

"可我知道，"吉姆说，"那是一只红盖子的背篮，里面

full of wonderful things."

"I said so," cried the bearer of the basket. "Do you think it will betray us?"

"Not if it is given to me. I can draw out the magic."

They arranged and re-arranged their little plans for another hour, while Kim shivered with cold and pride.

A mile down the hill lay two half-frozen men, demanding an explanation from the Babu, who seemed upset and afraid. He explained that they were lucky to be alive. The coolies could not be recalled, and if the Rajah heard what they had done, would surely cast them into prison.

Their only hope was flight from the village, as advised by the Babu, who would dissolve into tears demanding why they had hit the priest. Ten steps would have taken Hurree to shelter and food of the nearest village, but he preferred this show, and sat crouched against a tree trunk, sniffing.

"Have you thought how we will look, wandering through these hills?"

"Have you no consideration for our baggage. The baggage! Everything we had secured! Our gains! Eight months' work! Do you know what it means? Oh! You have done well!"

They argued and Hurree Babu smiled. Kim was with the baskets and in it lay eight months' of labour. There was no

装有非常奇异的东西。"

"我就是这么说的，"背这只篮子的挑夫大叫了起来，"这只篮子会把我们出卖掉吗？"

"交给我就不会了，我会把它的魔法释放出来。"

他们用了整整一个小时反复推敲他们那些天真的计划。吉姆则浑身发抖，因为冷，也因为得意。

山下一里处，躺着两个冻得半僵的人，希望从巴布这里得到解释。巴布看上去魂飞魄散。巴布解释说，他们还能活着已经算是命大了。那些挑夫已经无法再次召回了。而且，如果王爷听说他们所做的一切，会把他们关进牢房的。

巴布建议他们唯一的出路就是不事张扬地逃过一个个村落，他还泪流满面地质问为什么洋人打了圣人。再走上十步，哈利尔就可到最近的村子里要吃要住。可是他宁愿忍受寒冷，蜷缩着靠在树桩上，凄切悲咽。

"你想过没有，山里东奔西蹿的不是让人笑话吗？"

"你就不考虑我们的行李！行李！完了！我们的收获！八个月的劳动！你知道那意味着什么吗？啊，你干得可真不错！"

他们互相指责，哈利尔暗自发笑。篮子在吉姆那里了。里面是八个月的劳动所得。没办法和那孩子联系，不过他是

means of contacting him, but the boy could be trusted.

"How well I arranged it," thought Hurree Babu. "How quick I have been. It was all worth it. Consider the moral effect upon these people. No papers — no written documents — and me to interpret for them. How I shall laugh with the Colonel!"

"We will send the food and the red-topped basket. Then if anything is not needed, the basket is not required!"

He pointed through the window. "This is the world's end."

Till dawn, hour after hour, the Lama stared at the wall, and from time to time he groaned. Outside the coolies, with the Ao-chung man as their leader, opened the Sahib's tinned foods and enjoyed the taste, and left the rest in the Shamlegh kitchen and left the red-topped basket for Kim. Then they disappeared.

Kim tilted the basket on the floor and out fell the survey instruments, books, diaries, letters, maps, and at the very bottom lay an embroidered bag covering a sealed and gilded document, such as one king sends to another.

"The books I do not want. The letters I don't understand, but Colonel Creighton will. They must all be kept. The maps — they draw better maps than me — of course. And especially the King's letter. That must be from Hila's or Bunar. Hurree Babu spoke the truth. By Jove! It is a fine loot. I wish Hurree could know. The rest can go out of the window."

228

可以信赖的。

哈利尔想："我安排得真好，我脑袋转得多快啊！真是值得。考虑一下对这些人所产生的道义影响吧！没有条约，没有文件，只有我来为他们解释。等到跟上校在一起时，我们一定要开怀大笑一场。"

"我们会送来吃的。还有那只红盖子背篮，要是没什么需要的话，也没必要留着了。"

坳昌挑夫朝窗外一指："这里就是世界的尽头。"

喇嘛目不转睛，面壁而观，时间一个钟头一个钟头地流逝，他不时呻吟叹息着。外面的挑夫们，由那个坳昌挑夫当头，打开洋大人的罐头食品，发觉特别可口。他们把剩下的留在山姆里格的厨房里，把红盖子的篮子给了吉姆，然后消失了。

吉姆把篮子往地上一倾，掉出了测量仪、书本、日记本、信件和地图。篮子的底部有一只绣花袋，套着一封密封烫金的文件，这就是郡王致郡王的那种。

"这些书不要，这些信嘛我看不懂，可是克莱顿上校会懂的，这些都要。地图呢——他们画得比我好——当然要——特别是郡王那封信。一定是希拉斯或本纳尔寄出的。哈利尔·巴布说得对。我的天！收获可真不小。要是哈利尔知道该多好……其他这些统统扔到窗外。"

He sorted out the written material and the maps and letters and put them aside, along with the pocketbooks. "The letters must go in my belt, with the King's document, and the others in the food bag."

The rest he packed and flung the basket a thousand feet below, the contents flying in all directions.

"Now how am I to tell Hurree Babu? And what am I to do? My old man is sick. I must tie up these letters or they will be sweated." Kim made a neat packet with the oilskin and packed away the books.

Kim tore a page from the notebook and with a pencil wrote the message. "I have everything that they have written, the pictures of the country, and many letters and maps — especially the King's letter. Tell me what to do. I am at Shamlegh — under the Snow. The old man is sick." He gave to the woman of the place they were sheltering.

"Say it is from the Son of the Charm. And ask if there is an answer."

The woman turned resolutely uphill, as the morning sun rose fifteen hundred feet above.

As the forenoon wore out, Kim's messenger returned as untired as she had set out.

他挑拣出每一份手稿，每一张地图，连同信件还有袖珍本，然后，把它们放在一边："那些文件和郡王的信件必须放进我的腰带里，其他的可以放进食物袋子里。"

他把不要的东西装进篮子里，然后扔到千尺悬崖之下，所有的东西四处乱飞。

"现在，我怎么告诉哈利尔·巴布，下一步我该做什么呢？我那老师父又病倒了。我必须把这些信件包扎起来，否则它们会受潮的。"吉姆用油布包了一个整齐的包裹，把书整理一下放在旁边。

他从笔记本上撕下一页，用铅笔写下信息："他们写的我都拿到了，这个地方的地图，还有许多信件，特别是那封郡王的信。告诉我下一步怎么办。我在雪山下的山姆里格。老人家病了。"他把他们正在住宿的地址给了那女人。

"告诉那位巴布是符咒之子给他的,并问他是否有答复。"

她毅然地转身上了山，一千五百英尺上方的朝阳已冉冉升起。

中午时分，吉姆的信到了。那女人跟出发时一样，毫不气喘。

Kim read the reply. "Got your message. Cannot get away from present company at now, but shall take them to Simla, then will rejoin you. Do not follow these angry gentlemen. Return by the same road you came, and will overtake you. Highly pleased about the letters being found due to my forethought."

"Holy One, he says, he will escape from those men and will return to us. Shall we wait a while at Shamlegh?"

The Lama drew out Wheel of Life, and laid it open.

Kim stared at the disfigured chart, torn from left to right — across the Houses of Desire and the human and animal world — to the empty House of the Senses.

"The arrow fell in the plains, not the hills. So what are we doing here? I do not know how long I shall live in this body. What can a hakim do?"

吉姆读着回信："来信收到，目前无法摆脱同伴，我会把他们带进西姆拉。之后，与你会合。不宜随发怒绅士同行。按原路返回就能跟上。亏我深谋远虑，那些信被找到让我甚为满意。"

"圣者，他说，他会逃离那些人，回来跟我们一起走。我们是不是在山姆里格等一会儿？"

喇嘛掏出那幅轮回图，展开。

吉姆注视着那张破损不堪的轮回图。从左到右成对角拉开一道裂纹——从纵欲宫开始，经过人、兽两个世界，延伸到六根空舍。

"箭是落在平原上，不是落在山区。这样的话，我们还待在这里干什么呢？我不知道我这副身子还能活多久。大夫能有什么办法呢？"

19

BACK TO THE PLAINS

K im turned to the Shamlegh woman. "It is my loss." He sighed deeply, "but my master had a vision and led by it, he turns from this village to the plains again."

"I wait for thee, chela," said the Lama, leaning against the doorpost.

"It is all well," said Kim. "The thin air weakens you. In a little while we go."

Up the valleys of Bushahr, the far-sighted eagles change direction as they see a blue and white umbrella. Under it hurries a Bengali, once fat, now thinned by the weather. He has received the thanks of the two foreigners having guided them skillfully to Simla. It was not his fault that in the mist they by-passed the telegraph office.

He rejoiced that he had been of help in saving the Sahibs from the anger of the villagers. He begged food and arranged accomodation, and forgot the blows. He asked for nothing

十九
返回平原

　　吉姆转向山姆里格女人："这是我的损失，"他深深地叹了一口气，"我师父，他得到显圣的引导，又想着要离开村子到平原去。"

　　"我等着你呢，弟子。"喇嘛依靠在门柱上说。

　　"没什么事，"吉姆说，"空气稀薄，让你觉得虚弱无力。过一会儿，我们就走！"

　　在布沙山谷，一目千里的老鹰围着蓝白相间的伞打转。伞下的孟加拉人疾步行走，他曾经肥头大耳，现在形销骨立，满面风霜。他刚刚领受了两个外国人的一番谢意，因为他轻松地把他们带到了西姆拉。在霭霭湿雾中，他们错过了电报站，那可不是他的错。

　　他为自己能尽自己所能把洋大人们从愤怒的乡民间救出感到高兴。他乞求食物，安排招待事宜，忘记曾挨过拳打，他不求什么，只要给他一张证明，说明他——莫罕得罗·拉

but a testimonial that he "Mohendro Lal Dutt, M.A. of Calcutta 'had done the state some service'."

They gave him a certificate praising his skill as a guide, full of courtesy and care. The Babu sobbed with emotion. He led them to the Mall Simla, and from there vanished like a dawn cloud on Jakko.

On the edge of the Doon, Mussorie well behind them, rests a worn out litter, with a sick Lama who seeks a river for his healing.

"Be patient. We will reach freedom together on the banks of the river, and then will look back on our lives."

Kim thought of the oil skin packet and the books in the food bag. If someone duly authorised would only take delivery of them, then the Great Game might play itself out, for all he cared. He was tired and hot in the head, and a cough that came from the *stomach* worried him.

"You are too tender towards me."

"Not that either. I have done something without consulting you. I have sent a message to the Kulu woman, that you are weak and need a litter. I should have done that in the Doon. We shall stay here till the litter arrives."

"I am content. She is a woman with a heart of gold, but a talker."

尔·杜特，加尔各答的硕士，也曾"为国效力"过。

他们真的给了他一张证明，赞扬他作为一个向导，既彬彬有礼，又万无一失。巴布感激涕零。他带领他们来到西姆拉分界带，此后，他便像贾科山上黎明时的一团云彩一样消失了。

在杜恩边上，莫苏里已被远远地抛在后面。瘦弱的喇嘛，在破旧的轿子里休息着，他在寻找一条能治好病的河。

"忍耐一下，我们会一起求得解脱的。那时你和我，在圣河的彼岸，将回首我们的一生。"

吉姆想到了那个油布包和食品袋里的本子。只要有个指定的人把它们取走，他便不在乎大游戏怎么继续进行。他累了，脑袋里热烘烘的，从腹部上来的咳嗽也让他不安。

"你待我真是太好了。"
"不好，我没跟你商量就做了一件事。我送信给库鲁女人，告诉她你很虚弱，需要一顶轿子。本来在杜恩的时候我就应该想到这一点。我们就待在这里等轿子过来吧！"

"我知足了，那女人是个热心人，就是话多了些。"

"O Holy One, my heart is heavy for my many carelessnesses towards you. I love you — and it is too late — "overcome by *fatigue*, strain and the weight beyond his years, Kim broke down and sobbed at the Lama's feet.

"I have lived on your strength. I have stolen your strength. We will go to the woman from Kulu, and you can run free till your strength returns."

So he petted and comforted Kim.

"You lean on me in the body, Holy One, but I lean on you for some other things. Do you know it?"
"I have guessed may be," and the Lama's eyes twinkled.
"We must change that."

The palanquin from the Kulu woman travelled twenty miles.

"We are here on serious matters. A sickness of the soul took me to the hills, and him a sickness of the body. I have lived upon his strength — eating him," said the Lama.

Kim staggered dizzily to a room with a cot, and slept at once. The Lama had forbidden him to do any service to him.

"My chela is a son to me."
"He who sleeps there said,"the Lama nodded at the shut

"圣者，我待你常有不周到的地方，我心里很不安。我爱你……一切都太迟了……"不堪忍受超过年龄的紧张、疲乏和重负，吉姆心力交瘁，扑在喇嘛脚边泣不成声。

"我是靠了你的力量活了下来,从你的身上偷来力量。我们这就去库鲁女人那里,那你就可以轻松一下,养养精神。"

他就这样轻轻拍打并安抚着吉姆。

"肉体上你是靠着我，圣者，可在其他事情上是我靠着你。你难道不明白吗？"
"我猜想过，也许吧。"喇嘛眼里闪着光。
"我们必须改变一下。"

库鲁女人派来的轿子走了二十英里的路程。

"我们有正事才来这里。在山里我的灵魂中了邪,他的肉体得了病。我就一直在依靠他的力量，消耗他的体力。"喇嘛说。

吉姆晃晃悠悠地走进一个放着张帆布床的房间,马上睡着了。喇嘛跟他说了, 今天什么也不用他服侍。

"我这弟子对我来说就像是儿子一样。"
"在那边睡着的那个人说的,"他朝着吉姆那紧闭的房间

door of Kim, "that you have a heart of gold — and he is in spirit my very 'grandson' to me."

"I will take over the boy, and dose him and stuff him with good food, and make him whole again. We old people still know something."

When Kim would open his eyes, aching in every bone, and tried to get up to go to the kitchen to fetch the Lama's food, he would find a veiled figure, at the door, and a manservant, who told him that he was on no account to do anything.

"You must not get your master's food. You must do nothing. You want a locked box to keep holy books? O,that's another matter. Heavens forbid I should come between a priest and his prayers. It shall be brought and you shall keep the key."

They pushed the box under his cot, and Kim shut away Mahbub's pistol, the oilskin packet, the books and diaries, with a groan of relief. For some reason their weight on his shoulders was nothing to their weight on his poor mind.

"Your sickness is uncommon in youth these days. The remedy is sleep and certain drugs," said the Sahib.

Kim was glad to give himself to the blankness that soothed him.

点点头，"你的心肠真好——他在精神上正是我的'孙子'。"

"那孩子就交给我，我会给他喂药，给他吃饭，让他完全恢复。我们老年人还是有两下子的。"

当吉姆全身酸痛、一睁开眼就要去厨房拿饭给师父时，却发现门边站着一个披纱丽头巾的人，一位男仆人告诉吉姆，他绝不允许做任何事情。

"你千万别给你师父拿饭，你什么也不用做。要一个上锁的箱子装经书？哦，那是另一回事。上天不容阻挠和尚念经！箱子会送来，钥匙你自己管。"

他们将柜子推到帆布床下。吉姆把马哈布的手枪、油布包着的书还有日记统统锁了进去。然后宽心地舒了一口气。不知为什么，这些东西在他肩上的重量比起在他心头的重量来说简直微不足道。

"这种病如今在年轻人当中已经很少见了。治病的药方就是睡觉，还得吃一些药。"老夫人说。

吉姆很高兴能享受一种自己一无所知的舒缓疲乏的手艺。

She arranged for a cousin's widow, to massage Kim's body — bone by bone, muscle by muscle, ligament by ligament and nerve by nerve. Soothed as if hypnotised, Kim fell into a deep sleep — lasting 36 hours.

Then she fed him, and the whole house became busy arranging for his food — meals, vegetables, fish and spices, milk and onions.

Kim sat up and smiled. The terrible sickness had dropped off like an old shoe.

"Where is my Holy One?" he demanded.

"Your Holy One is well. Do not worry. He keeps both eyes on you when he is not wading into our brooks."

"Mother, I owe my life to you. How shall I thank? ten thousand blessings on this house — "

"Thank the Gods as a priest if you want to, but thank me as a son, if you really care," she said-"the hakim is low-spirited these days."

"What hakim, mother?"

"The very Dacca man. He came here about a week ago, anxious for your health. He was very thin and hungry, so I gave orders to have him stuffed with food too."

"I would like to see him if he is here."

"I'll send him. At least he had the sense to get the Holy One out of the river."

"He is a very wise hakim."

"I'll call him, my son. Get up and see the world. This ly-

　　老夫人安排了一个表亲的遗孀给吉姆按摩,他的一根根骨头,一块块肌肉,一条条韧带,一根根神经都被揉捏得舒舒服服。他精神恍惚,渐渐进入了梦乡,一睡就是三十六个小时。

　　接着她给他吃的,因为给他安排食物,整个房子都忙碌起来,准备的食物有肉、蔬菜、鱼、香料、牛奶、洋葱。

　　吉姆坐起来,眉开眼笑。糟糕的疾病已像旧鞋子一样被远远抛在脑后了。

　　"我的圣者在哪里?"吉姆问道。

　　"你的圣者很好,别担心。只要他不在我们的河里走,他就盯牢着你呢。"

　　"妈,我这条命是你拣回来的。我该怎么谢你才好?愿你的家得到千福万祉。"

　　"作为僧人如果你想谢的话,就谢神明。可是你要真想谢我就应当像一个儿子一样谢我,"她说,"那大夫这些天来心情不好。"

　　"你说什么大夫,妈?"

　　"就是那个达卡人。一星期前他来了,很为你的身体感到不安。他又饿又瘦,我就吩咐下人让他饱餐了一顿。"

　　"他要是还在这里,我想见见他。"

　　"我这就去叫他,至少他还有头脑把圣者从河里捞出来。"

　　"他是个很有头脑的大夫。"

　　"我会去叫他,我的孩子。起来看看这世界!老这么躺

ing in bed is the mother of seventy devils."

Soon the Babu walked in, with new shoes, and full of joy and greetings and looked well-fed.

"By Jove, Mister O'Hara, I am very glad to see you. I will kindly shut the door. It is a pity you are sick. Are you very sick?"

"The papers — the papers from the basket. The maps and the king's letter!" He held out the bag impatiently. The present need of his soul was to get rid of the loot.

"You are quite right. That is correct departmental view to take. You have got everything?"

"Everything that was handwritten I took. The rest I threw down the hill." Kim heard the turning of the key in the lock and the papers being pulled out.

He had been amazed that they lay below him through his sick days — a burden that could not be exposed.

"This is fine! This is the finest! Mr O'Hara. You have got the whole bag of tricks. They told me it was eight months' of work gone up in smoke. How they beat me! These are very clever maps. The *correspondence* proves that three or four prime ministers are involved. The British Government will put new kings on the thrones of Hila's and Bunar."

"Are they all in your hands?" said Kim. It was all he cared for.

244

着会生百病的。”

不一会儿，巴布就进来了，脚上穿着新鞋，肥滚滚的，满面春风。

“好家伙，欧哈拉先生，见到你真是太高兴了。我会关上门。真遗憾你病了。病得很重吗？”

“那些文件——背篮里拿出来的文件。地图还有郡王的信！”他迫不及待地一把掏出钥匙：他现在一心只希望尽快摆脱那些赃物。

“你做得对极了。这就是我们应该采取的务实态度。你全都拿了吗？”

“篮子里手写的东西我都拿了，剩下的我全丢到山下。”只听见钥匙插进锁孔旋转的声音，文件拿了出来。

吉姆惊讶于在他生病的这些日子里，一个不可告人的秘密就这样躺在他的下面。

“很好！太好了！欧哈拉先生，你已把他们一网打尽了。他们告诉我八个月的血汗全完了！他们把我打得多狠哪！这些地图画得很仔细，信件表明三四个首相卷入其中。英国政府要更换希拉斯和本纳尔的王位继承权，任命新的王位继承人。”

“信都在你手里吗？”吉姆关心的只是这点。

"I am going off directly. Mr Lurgan will be a proud man. Officially, you are below me, but I will include your name in the report. It is unfortunate that we are not allowed to make written reports." He tossed the key back.

"Good. I was very tired. My Holy One was sick too. Did he fall into — "

"Oh yes. I am his good friend, I tell you. He was behaving strangely, when I came down after you. I thought he might have the papers, so I followed him on his meditations. I found him just walking into the stream. He was nearly drowned, but for me. I pulled him out."

"Because I was not there!" said Kim. "He might have died."

"Yes, he might have, but he is dry now. You must make haste and come to Simla, and I will tell you my tale at Lurgan's. Mahbub Ali is here. He will see you soon."

"是的，我马上就走。勒甘先生会得意扬扬。编制上你是我的下属，不过在口头报告里我会提到你的名字。很遗憾不许我们写书面报告。"他把钥匙扔了回来。

"好，我好累。我的圣者又病倒了，他还掉进——"

"噢，是的。我是他的好朋友，我告诉你。我下山来找你的时候，发现他的举止很古怪，我想说不定文件在他那儿。他修习禅定时我跟在他身后，后来，他走进河里，要不是我的话，他都快淹死了，是我把他拉了出来。"

"都是因为我不在那里，"吉姆说，"他差点被淹死。"
"是啊，差点淹死，不过他现在身上全干了。你必须快点好起来，回去西姆拉，在勒甘那里我会把我的故事全说给你听。马哈布·阿里在这里，他会马上来看你。"

20

KIM'S RECOVERY AND THE SEARCH ENDS

All Kim felt he could not put into words. But he knew that his soul was disturbed. He looked upon the trees and the broad fields, and the thatched huts — his eyes felt strange, unable to take up the size and proportion of these things.

"I am Kim. I am Kim. And what is Kim?" His soul repeated again and again.

He did not want to cry, but of a sudden stupid tears trickled down — and slowly the things slid into proportion. Roads were meant to be walked upon — houses to be lived in. They were all real and true. He shook his head, and rambled out of gate.

"Let him go. I have done my share. Mother Earth must do the rest. When the Holy One comes back from meditation, tell him."

二十

吉姆康复 寻求终结

　　吉姆感觉他用语言表达不出来,但他知道他的心灵不能安宁。他抬头看看树木,再看看广阔的田野,还有茅草屋。他的眼睛变得很奇怪,不再能判断所见事物的大小、比例。

　　"我是吉姆。我就是吉姆。可吉姆是什么?"他的灵魂一遍一遍地重复这句话。

　　他并不想哭,可是突然之间,愚蠢的泪珠缓缓而下。慢慢地,物体又恢复了本来的大小、比例。道路是让人走的,房子是让人住的,他们全都是活生生、实实在在的。他甩了甩头,信步走出了大门。

　　"让他走走吧,我该做的都做了。剩下的该由大地母亲来做了。圣者经行回来时,告诉他。"老夫人说。

Bathed in the fresh air, his eyelids grew heavy as he neared it. The ground was good clean dust — though halfway to death — but holding the seeds of life. He laid himself down and Mother Earth breathed through him to restore him. His head lay powerless upon her breast, and his opened hands surrendered to her strength. The many-rooted tree above him knew what he wanted, though he did not know. Hour upon hour, he lay deeper in sleep.

Towards the evening, when the Lama and Mahbub Ali returned, they told them where Kim had gone.

"Allah! What a foolish trick to play in the open country. He could be shot a hundred times — but this is not the border."

"And," the Lama repeated again and again, "never was such a chela. Balanced, kind, wise, uncomplaining, cheerful on the road, truthful and polite. Great is his reward."

"I know the boy — as I have said."

"And he was all those things?"

"Some of them. But I have not found — yet, a Red Hat's charm for making him truthful. He has certainly been well-nursed?"

"Humph! I only wish the boy would come to no harm, and was a free agent. He and I were old friends in the first days of your pilgrimage together."

"That is a bond between us." The Lama sat down. "We are at the end of the pilgrimage. My time is short, I shall have safeguarded him throughout his years. He shall be free from sin when he quits his body."

吉姆的眼睑在清新的空气中显得沉重。好一片净土，尽管生命已经在通往死亡的途中，可还留有生命的种子。吉姆躺了下来，大地母亲的呼吸通过他的身体让他重新恢复。他把头无力地靠在她的胸脯上，展开的双手屈服于她的力量。他头顶上方那棵盘根错节的树都知道他在寻求什么，可他自己却一无所知。一个钟头又一个钟头地过去了，他就这么躺着。

将近傍晚时，喇嘛和马哈布·阿里来了，有人告诉他们吉姆去了哪里。

"真主啊，愚蠢的玩笑开到野外来了，他满可以挨一百发子弹的——幸亏这里不是边境。"

"而且，"喇嘛开始重复那套老生常谈，"从没见过这样的弟子。老成持重，和善可亲，有智慧，慷慨大方，一路上有说有笑，待人真诚，温文尔雅。他终获善果！"

"这孩子我了解——我就是这么说他的。"

"难道那时他就有这些优点？"

"其中的一些——不过我还没有见到哪个红帽喇嘛的符咒能让他变得真诚。他确实受到很好的教养。"

"嗬，我只想知道这孩子没受什么伤害，仍旧有自主权力。你们一同外出云游的初期，我和他就是老朋友了。"

"我和他之间有约定，"喇嘛坐了下来，"我们结束云游了。我的时间不多了，我会在他整个生命过程中一直保护他。他必须在生命结束之前清除罪孽。"

"How? Will you slay him, or drown him in your wonderful river? The babu dragged you from there."

"I was dragged from, no river. I found it by knowledge. To say I will take his life is sheer madness. My chela aided me to the River. It is his right to be cleansed of sin — with me. He must go forth as a teacher."

"Aha! Now I see. Certainly he must go forth as a teacher. He is somewhat urgently needed as a scribe by the State."

"He has been trained for that. He helped my search, I helped in his training. Let him be a clerk. What does it matter. He will reach Freedom at the end. The rest is illusion."

"This madman is fond of the boy, and I am reasonably mad too."Mahbub muttered.Aloud he said, "I must get to my horses. It grows dark. Do not wake him. My mind is easier now." With a tug at his belt, the Pathan swaggered off into the darkness.

"Wake! O fortunate — Wake ! It is found."

Kim came up from those deep wells, and the Lama enjoyed his yawn. He snapped his figures to head off evil spirits.

"I have slept a hundred years. Where — ? Holy One, have you been so long? I went out to look for you, but — slept — by the way. I am well now. Have you eaten? Let us go into the house. It is many days since I attended you."

"Gone — all gone. Do you not know?"

"你是要把他杀了，还是把他淹死在巴布把你拖出来的那条神奇的河里？"

"我根本不是从什么河里给拖出来的，真知领着我找到了那条河。说我要剥夺他的生命简直是荒唐。我的弟子帮助我找到了圣河。他有权利同我一道清除罪孽。他必须去当教员。"

"哈哈，现在我明白了！他是应该去当教员。国家很需要他去当个抄写员。"

"他原来就是准备当抄写员的。他帮助我寻找我的河，我也帮了他。让他去当个教员吧，有什么不好吗？他最终能获得解脱的。其他一切都不过是幻觉。"

"这疯子确实喜欢那孩子，这样说来我一定也够疯的。"马哈布低声嘟哝着，然后大声说，"我得去照顾我的马了。天黑了。别叫醒他。现在我轻松多了。"帕坦人扣上他的腰带，大摇大摆地走进了暮色中。

"醒来吧，幸运之子。醒来吧，它被找到了！"

吉姆从沉睡中被叫醒，喇嘛在一边怡然自得地打哈欠，一面还弹响手指，为他驱逐妖魔鬼怪。

"我睡了一百年。这是在哪里啊？圣——，你来很久了吗？我是出去找你的，可是——顺便提一下，我现在全好了。你吃过饭了吗？我们回那房屋吧。我有好多天没有照顾你了。"

"我全好了，什么病都没了。你还不知道吗？"

"Know what?" and Kim peered at the cross-legged figure, outlined like the stone Bodhisat.

"Hear me, I bring news. The search is finished. When we were among the hills, I lived on your strength. The young branch bowed and nearly broke. When we came out of the hills, I was worried for you and other matters which I held in my heart. The boat of my soul lacked direction. I could not see into the cause of things.

"So I gave you over to the virtuous woman. I took no food. I drank no water. I sat in meditation two days and two nights — breathing in and breathing out. Upon the second night — the reward came. My soul was freed from the silly body, and went free. It was a miracle!"

"A miracle, indeed."

"My soul went free, and flying like an eagle, saw there was no Teshoo Lama, nor any other soul. My soul drew near to the great soul, and I saw all India. I saw every camp and village where we had rested. I saw them at one time and in one place; for they were within the soul. By this I knew the soul had passed beyond the illusion of time and space and of things.

"Then my soul was alone, and I saw nothing, for I was all things. Then a voice cried, 'What will happen to the boy if you are dead?' and I was shaken with pity for you, and said, 'I will return to my chela, lest he should miss the way.' Then with great suffering, my soul, which is the soul of Teshoo Lama, separated itself from the great soul.

"知道什么？"他凝视着吉姆，盘腿坐着，那身影就像一尊菩萨的石像。

"听我说，有消息了！寻找结束了。我们在山里的时候，我看着你的力量，把嫩枝压得弯曲，差点折断。走出山区的时候，我又为你也为其他心头的事所烦恼。我的灵魂之舟迷失了方向。我无法探究万物因缘。

"所以我把你整个交代给那个好心的女人。我粒饭未进，滴水不喝，整整两天两夜。到了第二个晚上，善果来了，我的灵魂挣脱了愚蠢的身躯，无羁无绊。那真是个奇迹！"

"的确是奇迹。"

"我的灵魂了无羁绊，像老鹰似的飞旋，它看见既没有德寿喇嘛，也没有任何其他灵魂。我的灵魂慢慢地靠近一个伟大的灵魂。我看见了整个印度，我看了我们歇过的每一处营地。我在相同的时间看见这些地方同在一处，因为它们就在我的灵魂里。这时我知道我的灵魂已经超越了时间、空间和事物的幻觉。

"后来我的灵魂孑然独处，我便什么也看不见了，因为我就是一切。然后有个声音喊道，'你死后那孩子怎么办？'对你的怜悯使我内心把持不定，我便说，'我回去找我弟子免得他误了道。'接着，我的灵魂，也就是德寿喇嘛的灵魂，在极度痛苦中，奋力挣脱了大灵魂。

"At this moment a voice cried. 'The river! Take heed! The river!' — and I plainly saw the River of Arrow at my feet. But at that moment some evil held my arms and my waist. I pushed aside, but was held again in the body of Teshoo Lama, but free from sin. The hakim from Dacca bore me here. It is here. Behind the mango grove.

"The hakim was concerned about the Lama's body, and the horse seller came along with a cot, and carried me up to the Sahib's house. My search has ended. I found the river, break out at our feet. Now I am free of sin. Son of my soul, I have come to free you from all sin. Just is the Wheel. Our freedom is assured. Come." He crossed his hands on his lap and smiled.

　　"这时有个声音喊道：'那河！当心那河！'我清楚地看见箭河就在我的脚边。可那一刻，邪恶落在我的手臂上，缠绕住我的腰间，我把它甩到一边，我又套上了德寿喇嘛的身躯，可是一身清净无罪，达卡的大夫把我带到这里。那条河就在这片芒果林的后面——就在这里！

　　"那个大夫倒是很关心德寿喇嘛的身躯。马贩子带着帆布床来了，把我抬到老夫人家。我的寻找结束了。我发现了河，它在我们的脚边突然出现，现在我清净无罪了。我的灵魂之子啊，我来就是为了让你也清洗一切罪孽——正如生命之轮一样。我们肯定能得到超脱。来吧！"他双手交叉放在腿上，面含微笑。

词 汇 表

1

astride [əs'traid] *adv.* 跨坐地（的）；跨骑地
preference ['prefərəns] *n.* 偏爱；优先考虑；喜爱
rosary ['rəuzəri] *n.* 念珠；玫瑰园
curator [kjuə'reitə] *n.* 馆长
gravely ['grævəli] *adj.* 多碎石的；铺有碎石的
reverence ['revərəns] *n.* 崇敬；尊敬

3

stallion ['stæljən] *n.* 种马
pedigree ['pedigri:] *n.* 家谱；血统
amulet ['æmjulit] *n.* 护身符；驱邪符

4

virtue ['və:tju:] *n.* 高尚的道德；正直的品性
scruple ['skru:pl] *n.* 犹豫；顾忌
sabre ['seibə] *n.* （骑兵）军刀
contemptuous [kən'temptjuəs] *adj.* 傲慢的；轻蔑的

6

pretence [pri'tens] *n.* 虚假；假装；伪称
console [kən'səul] *v.* 安慰；慰问
penance ['penəns] *n.* 苦行；赎罪

8

document ['dɔkjumənt] *n.* 文件，公文；证件
colt [kəult] *n.* 雄驹；无经验的年轻人
intuition [,intju:'iʃən] *n.* 直觉力；直觉知识

9

wail [weil] *v.* 恸哭；大哭
calamity [kə'læmiti] *n.* 不幸之事；灾难
alms[a:mz] *n.* 善举；救济品；施舍；赈济

10

pacify ['pæsifai] *v.* 使镇定；安抚；平息
dye [dai] *v.* 染；把…染上颜色
worthwhile ['wə:θ'hwail] *adj.* 值得做的

11

hum [hʌm] *v.* 闭嘴哼唱；低唱
stroke [strəuk] *n.* （时钟等）鸣，敲；打击
errand ['erənd] *n.* 差遣；使命；任务
obese [əu'bi:s] *adj.* 肥胖的；胖嘟嘟的
betel ['bi:təl] *n.* （植物）蒌叶
handy ['hændi] *adj.* 有用的；便利的；在手边的

12

koran [kɔ'ra:n] *n.* （回教）古兰经
fortify ['fɔ:tifai] *v.* 加强；坚固；确证
turquoise ['tə:kwa:z] *n.* （矿物）土耳其玉
topside ['tɔp'said] *n.* 顶边；上端

13

croon [kru:n] *v.* 轻哼；低唱

scribe [skraib] *n.* 书记；作家；抄写员

spoke [spəuk] *n.* 轮辐，船舵轮柄

illusion [i'lju:ʒən] *n.* 错觉；幻影；幻想

14

strip [strip] *v.* 剥去；挤干（牛）奶；抢劫

jeer [dʒiə] *v.* 嘲弄；讥评

lounge [laundʒ] *v.* 闲逛，懒洋洋地靠着

assortment [ə'sɔ:tmənt] *n.* 分类；花色品种

16

pun [pʌn] *v.* 谐用双关语

encounter [in'kauntə] *v.* 遇见；遇上

sporting ['spɔ:tiŋ] *adj.* 有冒险性的；赌博性的

17

sullen ['sʌlən] *adj.* 闷闷不乐的；赌气的

invocation [,invəu'keiʃən] *n.* 祈祷；符咒；咒文

defile [di'fail] *v.* 亵渎；弄脏；弄污；玷污

19

stomach ['stʌmək] *n.* 胃；腹部

fatigue [fə'ti:g] *n.* 疲劳；疲乏

correspondence [,kɔris'pɔndəns] *n.* 通信；信件

Kim